Easy PC
wi-fi
networking

Other Computer Titles

by

Robert Penfold

Easy PC wi-fi networking

Robert Penfold

Bernard Babani (publishing) Ltd
The Grampians
Shepherds Bush Road
London W6 7NF
England
www.babanibooks.com

Please note

Although every care has been taken with the production of this book to ensure that any projects, designs, modifications, and/or programs, etc., contained herewith, operate in a correct and safe manner and also that any components specified are normally available in Great Britain, the Publisher and Author do not accept responsibility in any way for the failure (including fault in design) of any projects, design, modification, or program to work correctly or to cause damage to any equipment that it may be connected to or used in conjunction with, or in respect of any other damage or injury that may be caused, nor do the Publishers accept responsibility in any way for the failure to obtain specified components.

Notice is also given that if any equipment that is still under warranty is modified in any way or used or connected with home-built equipment then that warranty may be void.

© 2004 BERNARD BABANI (publishing) LTD

First Published - October 2004

British Library Cataloguing in Publication Data

A catalogue record for this book is available from the British Library

ISBN   0 85934 549 1

Cover Design by Gregor Arthur

Printed and bound in Great Britain by Cox and Wyman

Preface

The number of people that still swap data between computers using some form of disc is quite surprising. This method is perhaps understandable if there is a hundred miles between the two PCs, although there are still alternatives such as sending the files as Email attachments. It is less understandable when the two PCs are in adjoining rooms, or even in the same room. Many computer users have failed to grasp how easy and inexpensive it is to link PCs using a wired network.

Modern PCs are often supplied with a networking port as standard, and it is something that can be easily added to practically any PC. With two or more PCs connected into a network it becomes very easy to share files. In fact file sharing over a network is a built-in facility of Windows, and the shared files can be used much as if they were stored on the local PC. Printers can also be shared using Window's built-in networking facilities. A simple but very effective network can be produced without buying any additional software.

A common reason for potential network users sticking with their slow and inconvenient disc swapping is that they are reluctant to introduce any more cables into the building. Modern computers are generally equipped with a number of peripheral gadgets, each of which adds to the substantial amount of cabling associated with a basic PC. Networking cables trailing across the room, or through the building from room to room, is something that many computer users are not willing to give serious consideration to.

Fortunately, modern technology has come up with a solution in the form of wireless networking, or wi-fi as it is now called. Like many other technologies, the cost has dropped as it has become more widely used, and it no longer costs the proverbial "arm and a leg" to wirelessly network PCs. Some portable PCs are equipped with wi-fi adapters as standard, but wi-fi is easily added to practically any desktop or portable PC, including PDAs.

If you have three PCs in different rooms of a house they can now be linked without the need for any connecting cables. With the aid of wi-fi you can sit in the garden using a portable PC that not only links to the PCs in the house, but also shares their Internet connection. With the aid of wireless hotspots, you can even access the Internet using wi-fi when travelling around the world. Wi-fi is certainly one of the most exciting and useful developments in recent years, and it is a technology that can be of real benefit to most computer users.

Robert Penfold

Trademarks

Microsoft, Windows, Windows XP, Windows Me, Windows 98 and Windows 95 are either registered trademarks or trademarks of Microsoft Corporation.

All other brand and product names used in this book are recognised trademarks, or registered trademarks of their respective companies. There is no intent to use any trademarks generically and readers should investigate ownership of a trademark before using it for any purpose.

Contents

3

Practical wi-fi 69

4

Installation and security 95

5

Troubleshooting and optimising 153

Networking basics

Why use wires?

It is reasonable to question why a book about wireless networking should start with details of wired networks, or include wired networks at all for that matter. One reason is that there is a strong element of "learning to run before you can walk" if you dive straight in with wireless networking. It is much easier to learn about wireless networks when you already understand the basics of the wired variety.

Perhaps of more importance, few real world networks are based entirely on wireless connections. With a PC and a wireless modem/router on the same desk and less than a metre apart, a wireless connection could be used to link them. On the other hand, a lead costing a tenth as much will do the job just as well in this situation. In fact the lead will almost certainly permit faster communication and will avoid the security issues associated with wireless network connections. Do not use wireless links just for the sake of it. If a wired link is the more practical option, use one.

Network interfaces

In days gone by there were actually many different types of interface used in networking. The cheapest network systems relied on the standard PC serial or parallel ports, but they often provided nothing more than basic data swapping between two PCs. The rate at which data could be exchanged was quite slow. More recently a similar facility has been available using USB ports, but USB 1.1 ports are not very fast by networking standards, but high-speed transfers are possible using USB 2.0 ports.

The main drawback of these ultra-simple networking systems is that their expansion potential is strictly limited. In most cases it is nonexistent rather than limited, and they are only of use if you will never need anything beyond a simple link between two computers. Another drawback is that the cables tend to be relatively expensive, which negates the main point of using the computer's built-in ports. One of these basic links could actually cost more than using a "real" network. This will certainly be the case if your PCs have built-in network ports, and this is now quite a common feature

In the early days of PCs there were numerous interfaces designed specifically for networking, and some of these coexisted for many years. A standard network port gradually emerged as the Ethernet type became more popular and the others gradually "fell by the wayside". No doubt there are still many PCs that are networked by way of an alternative interface, but Ethernet is the only type that is currently in widespread use with PCs. If you have a PC with a built-in network port it will certainly be an Ethernet type, and it is the only networking method that will be considered in this book.

Ethernet ports are sometimes referred to as 10/100 networking ports. The two figures refer to the original speed of this interface and the speed of the improved version. They operate speeds of 10 and 100 megabits per second. Note that the speeds are in megabits per second and not megabytes. There are eight bits per byte, and with a practical networking system it is necessary to send more than just the raw data. Transfers at about 1 and 10 megabytes per second might be possible, but in practice it is likely that the transfer rates would actually be somewhat lower. Even being pessimistic about the performance of an Ethernet port, a 100 megabyte file could be transferred in less than 20 seconds, which is more than adequate for most purposes.

It is assumed here that the system can handle the higher operating speed, and any reasonably modern Ethernet port should be capable of doing so. When setting up a new network it is very unlikely that any 10-megabit equipment will be on offer from the retailers, and if any should be on offer it would definitely not be a good idea to buy it. Modern 10/100 Ethernet equipment costs so little these days that there is little point in bothering with old and inferior pieces of equipment. There is good compatibility between 10-megabit devices and the modern 10/100 variety, but as one would probably expect, a link only operates at the lower rate if one device is a 10-megabit type.

Note that 10 and 100-megabit cables are different. Although a 10-megabit cable will work with a 10/100 Ethernet system, it will only support operation at the slower rate. Again, the cost of a modern cable that operates at the higher speed is now so low that there is little point in using old 10-megabit cables. These days the 100-megabit cables are the only networking type that are likely available in the shops.

Adding ports

It might be necessary to install Ethernet ports in some of the PCs in the system, but the network has to be designed before a final decision can be made. As already pointed out, few practical wi-fi systems are totally wireless, but no Ethernet ports will be required if you should take this option. It might not be necessary to add any ports even if large parts of the system are cabled. Many PCs are supplied complete with an Ethernet port, and in the example of Figure 1.1 it is in the main cluster of ports, next to the USB types and below the PS/2 mouse and keyboard ports.

An Ethernet socket looks a bit like the type of telephone socket used in the USA and some other countries, and the sockets often used for broadband modems in the UK. Ethernet connectors are different though, and they are physically incompatible with any type of telephone

Fig.1.1 The Ethernet port is to the right of the two USB ports

socket. This is important, because some networking equipment has a socket to handle connections to telephone line or a modem. Using incompatible connectors ensures that errors are avoided when installing the cables. Ethernet equipment uses RJ-45 connectors, and the cables are sometimes referred to as RJ-45 cables.

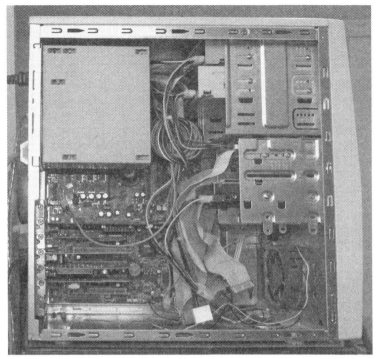

Fig.1.2 *Removing the left-hand side panel gives access to the expansion slots*

Modern laptop and notebook PCs often have an Ethernet port, but in a wi-fi system it would be normal to use the wireless option for any portable device. This avoids having to plug the computer into the system each time you return to base, and disconnect it again when you wish to go out with it again. Also, the wireless approach makes it possible to use the computer anywhere in the house, or even outside in the garden.

Adding an Ethernet port to a desktop PC is normally straightforward provided there is at least one PCI expansion slot free. The cost of generic Ethernet cards is extremely low, and those from the well-known manufacturers are not expensive. In order to add the card it is necessary to gain access to the interior of the PC, and this usually means removing the appropriate two or three screws at the rear of the unit. With some form of tower case this enables the left-hand side panel (as viewed from the front) to be pulled clear (Figure 1.2). Note that removing the other

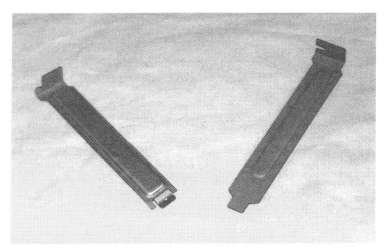

Fig.1.3 Two types of expansion port blanking plate

side panel will not give access to the expansion slots. With a desktop case it is the lid of the case that has to be removed.

There is usually a fair sprinkling of screws on the rear panel of the case, so look at the way the case is put together and be careful to remove the right ones. It is unlikely that any harm will be done if you should manage to remove one or two screws that (say) hold the power supply unit in place, but replace the screws immediately if a mistake is made. Fathoming some of the more stylish cases can be difficult, but if in doubt, the documentation supplied with the PC should explain how to gain access to the expansion slots.

Blanking plate

Before the network card can be fitted it is necessary to remove a blanking plate in the rear of the case for the particular slot you will be using. Cases used to be supplied with blanking plates that were screwed to a bracket at the rear of the case. This type is not used a great deal these days, but it is still to be found in some of the more up-market cases. Including screw-fixing type, there are three main forms of blanking plate currently in use.

The original type is held in place by a single screw per blanking plate. A bracket of this type is shown on the right in Figure 1.3. If you undo the

Fig.1.4 A new case that still has a full set of blanking plates

screw using a largish cross-point screwdriver the bracket should pull free without any difficulty. It is advisable to keep the bracket so the hole in the rear of the case can be blocked up again if you remove the expansion card at some later date. The bracket's fixing screw will be needed to hold the expansion card in place.

Probably the most popular kind of bracket these days is the type that is partially cut out from the rear of the case. In order to remove one of these it is necessary to twist it to and fro until the thin pieces of metal connecting it to the main casing fatigue and break. Figure 1.4 shows the rear of a new case with all of the brackets in place. In Figure 1.5 two of the brackets have been twisted round slightly to show how they can be broken away from the main casing. There is little point in keeping this type of bracket since it can not be fitted back in place again.

The third method has brackets that clip into the screw holes in the main case. A bracket of this type is shown on the left in Figure 1.3. These can be twisted slightly and pulled free, and the process is reversible provided the bracket is not seriously distorted during removal. It is therefore worthwhile keeping these brackets as they can be fitted into the case again should the need arise.

Fig.1.5 The plates can be twisted and eventually broken free

With the metal bracket removed, the network card (Figure 1.6) can be removed from its anti-static packing and pushed into position on the motherboard. Some cards and slots fit together quite easily while other combinations are less accommodating. Never try the brute force method of fitting expansion cards into place. Using plenty of force is virtually always the wrong approach when dealing with PCs, but it is certainly asking for trouble when applied to expansion cards. Apart from the risk of damage to the card itself there is also a likelihood of writing off the motherboard.

If a card seems to be reluctant to fit into place, check that the metal bracket is slotting correctly into place between the case and the motherboard. With some PCs the bottom end of the bracket has to be bent away from the circuit board slightly as it otherwise tends to hit the motherboard rather than fitting just behind it. Look carefully to see what is blocking the card. It can be quite dim inside a PC, so if necessary, get some additional light inside the PC using something like a spot-lamp or a powerful torch.

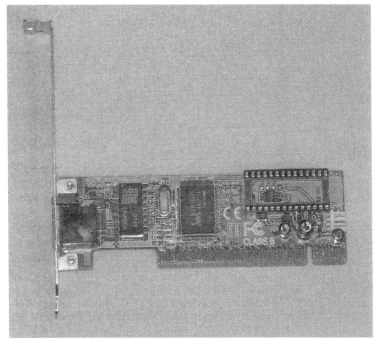

Fig.1.6 A PCI expansion card that provides an Ethernet port

Probably the most common problem is the card being slightly too far forward or back. This is the same problem with the metal bracket, but manifesting itself in a different manner. The bracket is fitting into place correctly, but the rest of the card is then out of alignment. If the misalignment is only slight, you should be able to ease the card backwards or forwards slightly and then into place.

Where there is a large error it will be necessary to form the bracket slightly in order to get the card to fit properly. In one or two cases where all else has failed, slightly loosening the screws that fix the motherboard to the chassis has provided the solution. Presumably in these cases the motherboard has been bolted in place when it is fractionally out of position. Loosening the mounting bolts and then fitting the expansion card shifts it into the correct position. The mounting bolts are then retightened, and fitting further expansion cards should be perfectly straightforward.

Fig.1.7 The expansion cards are bolted to the rear of the case

The mounting bracket can be fixed to the bracket at the rear of the case (Figure 1.7) once the card is correctly in place. Where appropriate, use the screw removed along with the blanking plate. It is otherwise a matter of looking through the odds and ends supplied with the PC, which should include at least one fixing screw per free expansion slot.

Although it is an Ethernet card that has been added in this example, the process is much the same for other PCI expansion cards. This includes PCI wi-fi adapters. One slight difference when installing a wi-fi card is that it usually has an aerial fitted on the bracket at the rear of the card. The aerial tends to get in the way when installing one these cards, so it is best to unscrew the aerial so that it is easy to fit the card in place. The aerial is easily fitted again once the card has been physically installed. Note that it is not a good idea to run any radio transmitting equipment without an aerial connected.

Shocking truth

If you are new to handling PC components it is important to realise that most of them, including practically all expansion cards, are vulnerable to damage from static charges. I think it is worth making the point that it does not take a large static charge complete with sparks and "cracking" sounds to damage sensitive electronic components. Large static discharges of that type are sufficient to damage most modern semiconductor components, and not just the more sensitive ones.

Many of the components used in computing are so sensitive to static charges that they can be damaged by relatively small voltages. In this context "small" still means a potential of perhaps a hundred volts or so, but by static standards this is not particularly large. Charges of this order will not generate noticeable sparks or make your hair stand on end, but they are nevertheless harmful to many electronic components. Hence you can "zap" these components simply by touching them, and in most cases would not be aware that anything had happened.

An obvious precaution when handling any vulnerable computer components is to keep well away from any known or likely sources of static electricity. These includes such things as computer monitors, television sets, any carpets or furnishings that are known to be prone to static generation, and even any pets that are known to get charged-up fur coats. Also avoid wearing any clothes that are known to give problems with static charges. This seems to be less of a problem than it once was, because few clothes these days are made from a cloth that consists entirely of man-made fibres. There is normally a significant content of natural fibres, and this seems to be sufficient to prevent any significant build-up of static charges. However, if you should have any garments that might give problems, make sure that you do not wear them when handling any computer equipment or components.

Static-sensitive components will be supplied in some form of anti-static packaging, and this is usually nothing more than a plastic bag made from a special plastic that is slightly conductive. There is quite a range of anti-static packaging currently in use, but an expansion card is unlikely to be supplied in anything more elaborate that a conductive plastic bag. This effectively short-circuits the edge connector of the card so that no significant voltage can build up between the terminals.

Although it is tempting to remove the components from the packing to have a good look at them, try to keep this type of thing to a minimum. Ideally it should be completely avoided. When it is necessary to remove

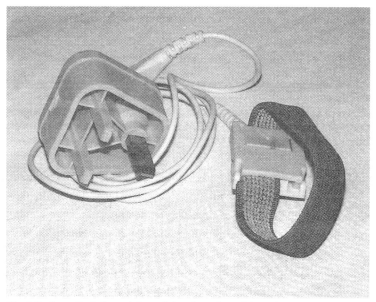

Fig.1.8 An anti-static wristband, lead, and earthing plug

the card from its packing, always make sure that both you and the plastic bag is earthed before the component is removed. Simply touching the earthed chassis of a computer while holding the component in its bag should be sufficient to ensure that everything is kept free of static charges.

The computer must be switched off and the power should also be switched off at the mains socket. The chassis of the computer will still be earthed provided the mains lead is connected to the computer and the mains socket. There is a risk of a charge gradually building up in your body, but touching the earthed chassis of the computer every minute or so will prevent this from occurring.

Wristbands

If you wish to make quite sure that your body remains static-free, you can earth yourself to the computer by way of a proper earthing wristband. This is basically just a wristband made from electrically conductive material that connects to the earth via a lead and a high value resistor. The lead is terminated in a clip that permits easy connection to the chassis

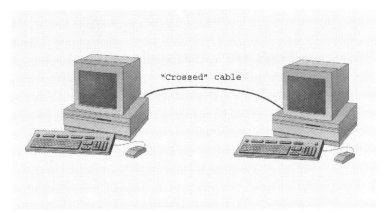

Fig.1.9 The most basic network consists of two PCs and no other equipment

of the computer. The resistor does not prevent any static build-up in your body from leaking away to earth, but it will protect you from a significant shock if a fault should result in the earthing point becoming "live". A variation on this system has a special mains plug that enables the wristband to be safely earthed to the mains supply. Earthing wristbands are available from some of the larger computer component suppliers, and from electronics component retailers.

A typical wristband, complete with lead and special earthing plug, is shown in Figure 1.8. Note that these are sometimes sold together as a kit, but they are also sold as separate items. Make sure you know what you are buying before you part with your money. The wristband on its own is about as much good as a monitor without the rest of the PC. It is possible to buy disposable wristband kits, but if you are likely to do a fair amount of PC upgrading from time to time it is probably worthwhile obtaining one of the cheaper non-disposable types. With intermittent use one of these should last many years. If you do not want to go to the expense of buying a wristband, the method of periodically touching the earthed chassis mentioned previously should be just as effective.

That is really all there is to it. Simply having a large chunk of earthed metal (in the form of the computer case) near the work area helps to discourage the build-up of any static charges in the first place. The few simple precautions outlined previously are then sufficient to ensure that there is no significant risk to the components. Do not be tempted to simply ignore the dangers of static electricity when handling computer components.

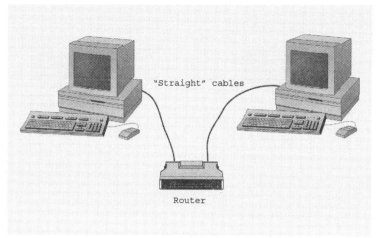

Fig.1.10 A basic network for two PCs that uses a router

When building electronic gadgets I often ignore static precautions, but I am dealing with components that cost a matter of pence each. If one or two of the components should be zapped by a static charge, no great harm is done. The cost would be minimal and I have plenty of spares available. The same is not true when dealing with computer components, some of which could cost in excess of a hundred pounds. Also, the computer would remain out of commission until a suitable replacement spare part was obtained.

Basic network

With all the PCs in the system equipped with Ethernet ports it is time to design and build the network. The most basic network barely justifies the "network" description, and it just consists of one PC connected direct to the other via their Ethernet ports (Figure 1.9). It is important to realise that Ethernet ports are not primarily designed for this method of connection, and this setup will not work if a normal network cable is used. The cable required when linking two PCs is usually called something like a "crossed" or "crossed-over" cable. A normal network lead is usually described as a "straight" cable.

The setup shown in Figure 1.10 is essentially the same as the one of Figure 1.9, and it provides a link between the two PCs. The PCs are

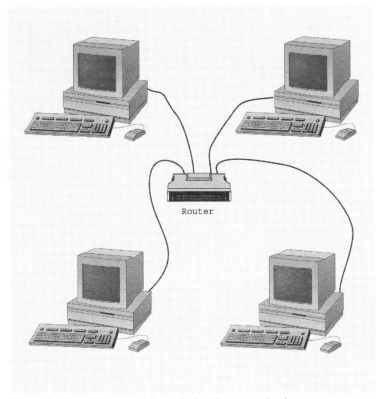

Fig.1.11 More PCs are easily added to the network. A router can
usually accommodate at least four PCs

linked via a networking router, and the two cables are of the "straight"
variety. In the arrangement of Figure 1.9 the crossed-over connections
in the cable makes each PC "look" like a router to the other PC. This
avoids the expense of the router and it is probably the better method if it
will never be necessary to introduce other computers into the system.

A big advantage of using a router is that it will typically have four or more
Ethernet sockets, making it easy to add further PCs into the network.
Figure 1.11 shows a network having four PCs, and the setup of Figure
1.10 is easily expanded into this configuration. It could probably use the
original router, since these mostly have four or more Ethernet sockets.
Therefore, the only additional hardware required would be two cables,
plus the two extra PCs of course. Networks can become quite involved,

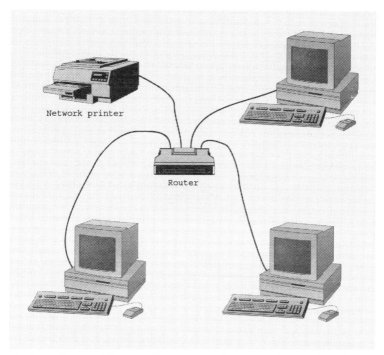

*Fig.1.12 Some printers can be connected direct to the router, and
used by any PC in the system*

but for a home or small business network it should not be necessary to
use anything more than a single router to bind the system together.

Shared resources

As described so far, the system contains nothing other than the
networking equipment and the PCs. This is fine for sharing files and
folders, and a basic twin PC network is often used for games that can
accommodate two players using separate PCs. However, most users
wish to go beyond data sharing. Other resources can be shared, and in
practice this usually means sharing a printer and/or an Internet
connection.

Some printers are network enabled, which basically just means that they
have an Ethernet port and can be connected into the system as in Figure

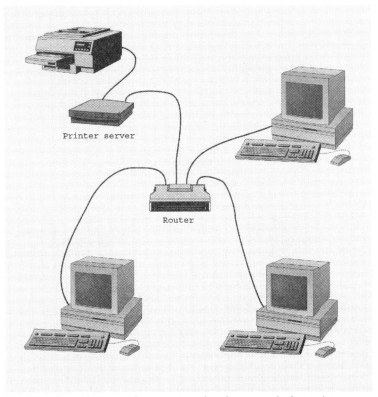

*Fig.1.13 Any printer can be connected to the network via a printer
server*

1.12. Heavy-duty printers for business use often have an Ethernet port
as standard, and it should certainly be available as an option. It is not
included as standard with the printers used in most home and small
business systems, and will probably not be available as an optional extra
either.

With the aid of a suitable gadget it is possible to connect practically any
printer into the network via the router, but it is not usually cost-effective to
use this method. The gadget is called a printer server, and it simply
goes between the router and the printer (Figure 1.13). Real-world printer
servers often have the ability to drive more than one printer. This method
has the major advantage of making the printer or printers available at all
times to any network user. Furthermore, it does so without increasing

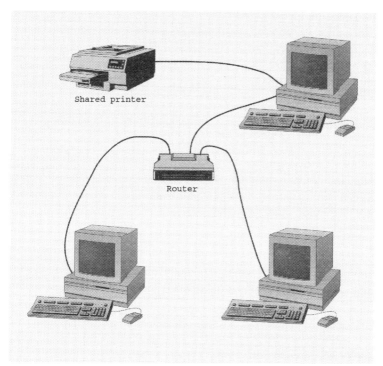

Fig.1.14 Any printer can be shared without using any extra equipment

the workload of any PCs that are not accessing a printer. The only real drawback is that cost of a printer server is greater than that of many inkjet printers. These days it can even be higher than the cost of a budget laser printer.

The more common approach with small networks is to install the printer on one of the PCs in the usual way (Figure 1.14). The printer can then be designated as a shared resource and made available to any PC on the network. This system works well in most respects, but it does have one slight drawback. The printer will only be available to the network when the PC it is connected to is switched on. A printer that has its own network connection is available to the system at all times, as is one driven via a printer server.

With the setup of Figure 1.14 it can be necessary to switch on one PC so that another one can use the printer. Another slight drawback is that the

PC which drivers the printer has an increase in its workload when other PCs access the printer. Even so, this method is still the most practical for most home and small business networks.

Internet sharing

Sharing an Internet connection is probably the main reason for home and many small business users organising their individual PCs into a network. However, it is only fair to point out that sharing an Internet connection does not work well with an ordinary dialup connection. In practice, a 56k modem is unlikely to achieve transfer rates of 56k, since this figure assumes a technically perfect connection. A technically perfect connection is unlikely to be achieved even if you happen to live next door to the telephone exchange.

In real-world computing a connection rate of about 48k is typical, and in some areas even this might not be achievable. A rate of 48k is not particularly fast with one person using the connection, and it becomes painfully slow when shared between (say) three people. When all three use the Internet simultaneously they have an effective connection rate of just 16k each.

It is generally considered to be more practical for each computer to be connected to the Internet via its own modem, with users taking it in turns to use the Internet. This requires one modem per computer and a telephone socket for each modem. However, most PCs have a modem as standard, and most premises are now well equipped with telephone sockets. Any extra hardware required is likely to be cheap, but in most cases it will not be needed.

Sharing broadband

The situation is very different with broadband, where connection speeds are much greater. A standard ADSL broadband connection has a download speed of 512k. The download speed in fringe areas is less than this, but for most broadband users the download rate is at least the stated 512k. This is at least ten times faster than the actual connection rate achieved with most 56k modems. Three users accessing the Internet simultaneously would each have an effective connection speed of just over 170k. In other words, they could still connect to the Internet at a rate more than three times better than a single user with a 56k modem.

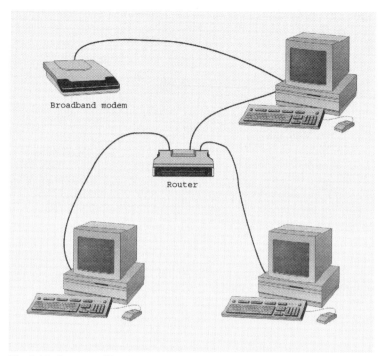

Fig.1.15 A system like this enables a modem and Internet connection to be shared

It is only fair to point out that some broadband providers have terms of service that limit or ban the sharing of a broadband connection. It is unlikely that you will encounter any restriction of this type with a broadband package aimed at business users, but there are often "strings attached" to the low-cost deals for home users. The self-install broadband packages often have restrictions, and in some cases there is an outright ban on shared connections.

Pressure from users and widespread flouting of the rules has led to some easing of the restrictions. Many providers now permit sharing between two or three users, but anything beyond this is likely to be outside the terms of service for low-cost broadband deals. Sharing a broadband connection between two or more households is unlikely to be permitted.

One way of sharing a broadband connection is to have the modem connected to one PC, with the Internet connection then being designated

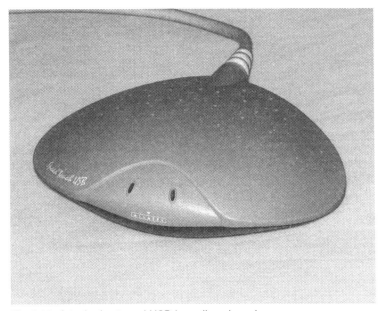

Fig.1.16 A typical external USB broadband modem

as a shared resource. This gives a setup of the type shown in Figure 1.15. Broadband modems are available in the form of PCI expansion cards, but the external USB type (Figure 1.16) is probably more popular.

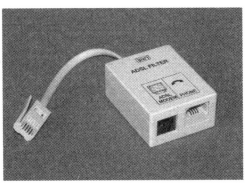

Fig.1.17 The most common type of microfilter

This method of sharing a broadband connection is cheap and easy if there is an existing network. You need little more than the modem and a microfilter for each telephone socket. The microfilters are needed to prevent the normal audio telephone signal from interfering with the high frequency broadband signal, and vice versa.

A microfilter usually has a short lead that plugs into the telephone socket, and a couple of sockets on the main unit (Figure 1.17). One socket is for a telephone and the other is for the broadband modem. You can also obtain microfilters that look rather like a two-way telephone adapter (Figure 1.18), but one

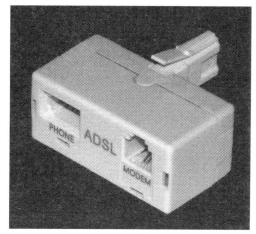

Fig.1.18 An alternative form of microfilter

of the sockets is for a broadband modem. Note that it is normally necessary to have a microfilter per telephone socket, and not just one filter at whichever socket happens to be used with the modem.

Microfilters

It is possible to use an ordinary modem with a telephone line that is broadband enabled, but the modem must be used via the ordinary telephone socket of a microfilter. It is possible that the filter will produce some loss of performance, although no problems were evident when I tried using a modem with two different microfilters. Although it is unlikely that you would need to use a dialup connection when a broadband type is available, an ordinary modem might still be needed for sending and receiving faxes. Also, it is a good idea to have a dialup connection available as a backup in case the broadband connection fails for some reason. Obviously the backup will be no use either if the lines goes "dead", but it does sometimes happen that the broadband connection is inaccessible while the line works fine in other respects.

A rather different scheme of things is normally used for a broadband connection that is installed by an engineer. The engineer usually installs a box that has an Ethernet socket on the front, and this is connected into the network by way of a suitable router. The ordinary telephone connections are left unchanged, and they do not require the use of

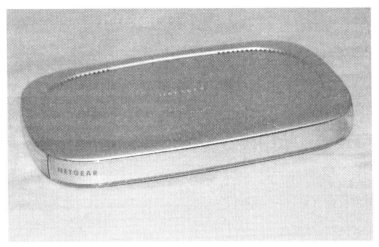

Fig.1.19 A combined router and ADSL broadband modem

microfilters. There is no exact equivalent of this for self-install systems, but it is possible to obtain a broadband modem that has an Ethernet socket for connection to the network. With this arrangement a microfilter is still required at each telephone socket.

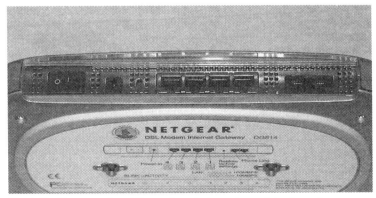

Fig.1.20 There are four Ethernet sockets and one telephone type

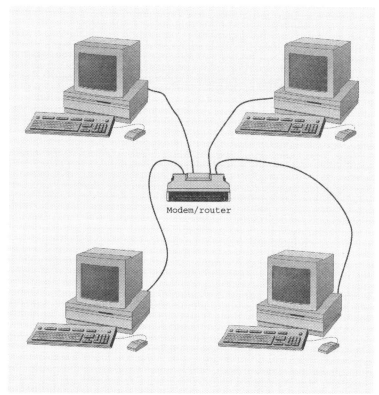

Fig.1.21 This is the most convenient method of sharing an Internet connection

Modem/router

Probably the most popular means of sharing a broadband connection between a few computers is to use a combined modem and router, such as the one shown in Figure 1.19, which has four Ethernet sockets on the rear panel (Figure 1.20). There is also a telephone socket which is connected to a telephone wall socket via a microfilter. A combined modem and router is used in a setup of the type shown in Figure 1.21. This is basically just a standard network, but with the important difference that any PC connected to the router is automatically provided with Internet access. It is possible to obtain much the same effect using a separate router and broadband modem (Figure 1.22), but combining the two units gives a neater solution.

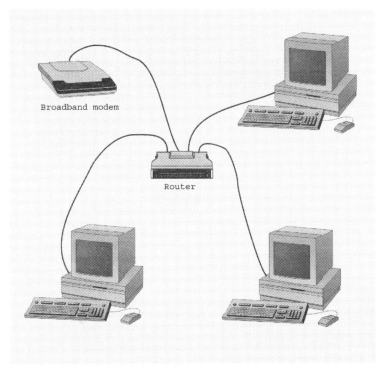

Fig.1.22 An alternative method of sharing an Internet connection

If you decide to use a setup like the one in Figure 1.22, bear in mind that you can not use any broadband modem with any router. The router must be one that is designed to be used in this way. Also, most routers have an Ethernet socket for the modem, and can only be used with modems that have an Ethernet socket. It could be difficult to track down a router that will work with a modem that only has a USB interface.

Using a gadget that combines a router and modem, possibly with a firewall or other functions, is certainly the best method. Setting up the network is generally much easier using an all-in-one solution, and it helps to reduce the amount of cabling. Most wireless networks have wired connections as well, but you must avoid having the wireless name become ironic! Try to keep everything neat and simple, with no more "boxes" and cables than is really necessary.

An advantage of the current low prices of computer hardware is that it is usually possible to design a system that accurately matches your requirements, rather than having to compromise due to cost considerations. Depending on the equipment you have to start with, a setup of the type shown in Figure 1.21 might cost a little more than one like Figure 1.15. The cost is likely to be small though, and the arrangement of Figure 1.21 is much better from the users' point of view.

With the setup of Figure 1.21 the modem/router is usually left running continuously, making an Internet connection always available to any PC in the network. With the arrangement of Figure 1.15 it is necessary to have the right PC switched on in order to access the Internet using any of the others. Another point to bear in mind is that the PC connected to the modem becomes a form of router, and this will place additional claims on its resources. Using a modem combined with or connected to the modem avoids any overhead on any of the PCs in the system. All the additional workload is handled by the router.

In the past it was common for an old PC to be given a new lease of life by using it to operate as a router or router/modem. This might appear to be a very environmentally friendly way of doing things, but it is less "green" than it seems. A modern router or modem/router consumes little power, and costs little to run. A PC has a much higher power consumption, and if left operating for long periods every day will soon run up significant running costs. In the long term it is likely to cost much more than buying a new router or modem/router.

Firewalls

In addition to those already mentioned, there are a few more practical differences between using an arrangement of the type outlined in Figure 1.21 and one like Figure 1.15. In practice it is usually easier to configure the arrangement of Figure 1.21, because the Internet connection will be automatically shared between the PCs in the system. With the setup of Figure 1.15 the modem is a resource of one PC, and it will only be shared if it is designated as a shared resource, which requires some additional setting up.

Perhaps of greater importance, the setup of Figure 1.21 gives greater security. It is worth making the point that security is now an important issue for all Internet users, but it is of even greater concern for broadband users. Some form of firewall to keep hackers at bay should be considered essential rather than an optional extra for a broadband connection. A firewall can be either a piece of hardware or a program. A firewall's basic function is much the same whether it is implemented in software or hardware.

Some people seem to think that a firewall and an antivirus program are the same, but there are major differences. There is often some overlap between real world antivirus and firewall programs, but their primary aims are different. An antivirus program is designed to scan files on discs and the contents of the computer's memory in search of viruses and other potentially harmful files. Having found any suspect files, the program will usually deal with them. A firewall is used to block unauthorised access to your PC, and in most cases it is access to your PC via the Internet that is blocked. Bear in mind though, that a software firewall will usually block unauthorised access via a local area network (LAN) as well.

Of course, a firewall is of no practical value if it blocks communication from one PC to another and access via the Internet. To be of practical value it must only block unauthorised access to any part of the system. When you access an Internet site your PC sends messages to the server hosting that site, and these messages request the pages you wish to view. Having requested information, the PC expects information to be sent from the appropriate server, and it accepts that information when it is received. A firewall does not interfere with this type of Internet activity provided it is set up correctly.

It is a different matter when another system tries to access your PC when you have not instigated the initial contact. The firewall will treat this attempted entry as an attack and will block it. Of course, the attempt at accessing your PC might not be an attack, and a firewall can result in legitimate access being blocked. Something like P2P file swapping is likely to fail or operate in a limited fashion. The sharing of files and resources on a local area network could also be blocked. A practical firewall enables the user to permit certain types of access so that the computer can work normally while most unauthorised access is still blocked. However, doing so does reduce the degree of protection provided by the firewall.

Broadband risks

As pointed out previously, using a firewall is considered to be much more important when using some form of broadband Internet access. One reason for this is simply that with a high-speed connection it will be less obvious if someone is accessing your PC. With a slow dial-up connection the additional flow of data would slow things down and be more readily apparent. Another, and perhaps more important reason, is that with most types of broadband connection you are provided with a fixed Internet address. Having found your PC it is possible for a hacker to go back to it again whenever it is switched on. With a dial-up connection your Internet service provider (ISP) normally provides a new Internet address each time you logon to their system.

Another point to bear in mind is that with a broadband connection the PC is usually connected to the Internet all the time that it is operating, and not just when you decide to go online and do some surfing. With many PCs this means that there is a connection to the Internet virtually all day every day. Even if you are provided with a new Internet address each time the PC is switched on, it will probably be operating with that address for many hours before it is switched off again. This still leaves it relatively vulnerable to attack.

With some types of modem the Internet connection does not close down when the PC is switched off. The modem remains connected to the Internet all the time unless it is switched off, which most users do not bother to do. Quite reasonably, they would like the Internet connection to be ready for use whenever any PC in the system is switched on. With the modem left running, the system retains the same address for what could easily be weeks or even months. Strictly speaking, this does not give the system a permanent address, but it does provide hackers with plenty of opportunities to return to your computer system.

Built-in firewall

A combined router and modem provides what is effectively a built-in hardware firewall. The router ensures that the received data is sent to the correct PC. It also ensures that any data sent from one PC is kept separate from any data from the other PCs. The router uses a process known as network address translation (NAT), and it provides the firewall action as a by-product of the sharing process.

The only device in the system that can be recognised externally is the router. Anything on the other side of the router is "invisible" to the outside world. The router uses the real Internet address provided by your ISP, but the PCs in the system use a sort of fake address based on the real one. The router makes the necessary adjustments to incoming and outgoing data so that everything runs smoothly.

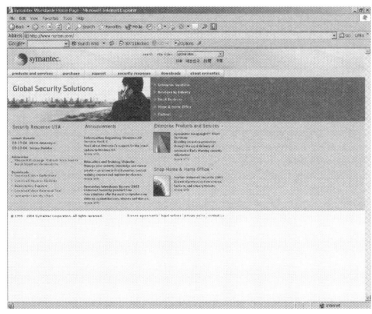

Fig.1.23 The Norton.com homepage

Many combined firewall and routers additionally have a system known as Stateful Packet Inspection (SPI). This keeps track of incoming and outgoing packets of data to check that incoming packets are genuine replies to outgoing requests. If a hacker should manage to find a way through the router, this system should ensure that their fake packets of data are detected and ignored.

I tested the firewall capability of a Netgear DG834G by going to a couple of websites which run tests that are supposed to shock you by showing how vulnerable your PC is to Internet attacks. The first site tried various methods of attacking the system but was unable to access any of the PCs in the network. In fact it was unable to detect a computer at the appropriate Internet address. Results were much the same at the second site. This lack of success was due to the fact that the system at the test site was "talking" to the router and not the PCs on the other side of the router. There is no point in trying to hack into a PC that is not there.

Security is obviously important for all Internet users, but it is especially important for anyone that has a network connected to the Internet via a broadband connection. You are potentially providing hackers with a

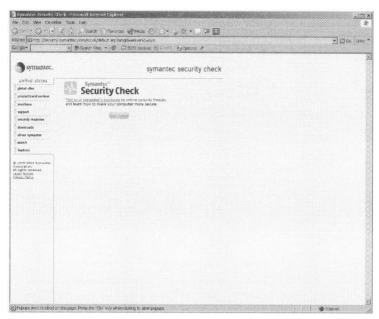

Fig.1.24 Operate the Go button to move on to the next stage

high-speed link into all the PCs in the system. It is a good idea to use one of these test sites on a newly installed or upgraded network, just to make sure that hackers have no easy way into the network. Make sure that you use one that is provided by a reliable source. Spoof sites of various types seem to be a growing threat on the Internet.

Probably the best know of the test sites is the one run by Symantec, the producers of the Norton range of security software and other utilities. The home page for their site (Figure 1.23) is at:

www.norton.com

The Symantec Security Check link is in the Downloads section near the bottom left-hand corner of the page. This produces the brief information page shown in Figure 1.24. Press the Go button to move onto the next page (Figure 1.25) where a security scan or a check for viruses can be made. In this case it is the security scan that is required, and the appropriate Start button is operated. The check then begins, and a page with a bargraph display shows how things are progressing (Figure 1.26). Online virus scans take minutes or even hours, but this type of check is

Fig.1.25 It is the Security Scan option that is selected here

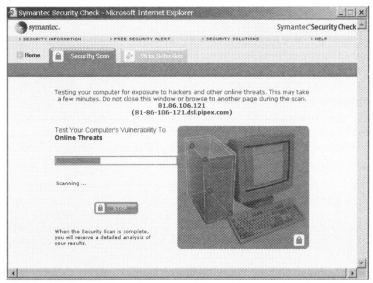

Fig.1.26 The check is underway, and should be completed quickly

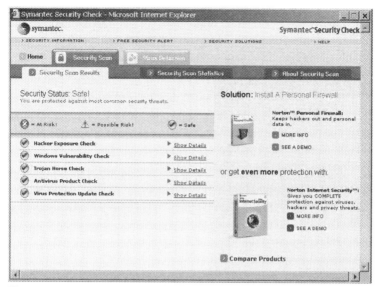

Fig.1.27 This network has passed all the tests

quite fast. After a minute or so the list of results should be displayed (Figure 1.27). The top three checks in the list are the ones that are of interest in the current context, and a basically secure system should pass all three.

It is unlikely that the barrier provided by a router, or any other type of firewall for that matter, can ever be one hundred percent effective against hackers. However, it certainly makes it very difficult to hack into one of the PCs in the system. This is probably all you need to do in order to avoid attacks from hackers. If your PC system proves to be difficult to penetrate it is likely that any hackers will go elsewhere in search of easier pickings.

Additional firewall

The firewall action provided by a router is quite effective, but it can still be beneficial to have an additional firewall. This can be provided by a program running on the PC, but some combined modems and routers have a "proper" firewall built in. If you need firewall software, there are a number of well known firewall programs available, and a program of this type is sometimes included in suites of utility programs. A firewall program is sometimes included with network hardware such as a router/modem. Fortunately, personal firewall programs, unlike the highly sophisticated business firewalls, are reasonably inexpensive. In fact one or two free firewall programs are available. Software firewalls all operate in essentially the same manner and use the same techniques.

One of these techniques is to monitor Internet activity and alert the user if a non-authorised program tries to access the Internet. Initially there might be alerts when running programs that involve legitimate Internet access, but once you have set up the firewall to recognise legitimate Internet traffic this should no longer be a problem. This form of monitoring is guarding against software such as Trojans and spyware, that try to send information obtained from your PC to another system on the Internet.

A basic hardware firewall will not guard against this type of thing, because it will consider any Internet access that originates from your PC to be legitimate. A software firewall that provides this type of monitoring will detect and block Internet activity from any program that you have not granted Internet access. Although a basic hardware firewall is very good at guarding against external attacks, it will not prevent an internal attack if you should download a Trojan or similar program. For the ultimate in security a hardware firewall therefore has to be backed up by appropriate software protection.

Another technique used by software firewalls is essentially the same as the SPI facility provided by some combined modem and routers. The vast majority of incoming messages are in response to a request sent from the PC. The firewall inspects received packets of data and blocks them unless they are the result of a request for data sent by the PC. Of course, a facility of this type provided by a software firewall is superfluous if you are using a combined modem and router that incorporates SPI, as it just duplicates an existing feature

Whether implemented in software or hardware, this method gives excellent security, but some facilities might be lost because they require the initial contact to come from the remote system. For example, any form of P2P network is likely to operate in a restricted fashion. Like hardware firewalls, the software variety normally has a facility that permits exceptions to be specified so that these facilities can be reinstated.

Ports

When dealing with firewalls you are almost certain to encounter the term "ports". In a computer context this normally means a socket on the PC where a peripheral of some kind is connected. In an Internet context a port is not in the form of any hardware, and it is more of a software concept. Programs communicate over the Internet via these notional ports that are numbered from 0 to 65535. It enables several programs to utilise the Internet without the data for one program getting directed to another program.

Software and hardware firewalls usually have the ability to block activity on certain ports. The idea is to block ports that are likely to be used by programs such as backdoor Trojans but are not normally used for legitimate Internet traffic. A backdoor Trojan could be set to "listen" on (say) port 80, and send the data it has collected once it receives a message from a hacker. By blocking any activity on port 80, the firewall ensures that the backdoor Trojan can not send any data, and that it will not be contacted in the first place.

Using this method gives a basic hardware firewall some ability to combat backdoor Trojans, spyware, and other attacks that originate from within the system. If a program is designed to collect information from your PC and send it via a particular port, blocking that port will defeat the program. Clearly it is not possible to block all ports, but blocking those that are often used by "spy" programs gives an improvement in security.

Note that most software firewall programs will block this type of activity anyway, because the firewall will detect that an unauthorised program is trying to use the Internet. It will alert the user and only permit the data to be sent if the user authorises it. Presumably the user would "smell a rat" and deny permission for the Trojan to access the Internet. Where a trigger message is required, most hardware firewalls would prevent the message from the hacker from reaching the Trojan, and would also prevent the attack from succeeding. Even so, it is useful to block ports that are likely to be used for hacking the system. Doing so makes it that much harder for someone to "crack" your system, which is what Internet security is all about.

False alarms

Many of the early firewall programs had a major problem in that they were a bit overzealous. While you were trying the surf the Internet there were constant interruptions from the firewall informing you of attacks on the system. In reality these attacks were wholly or largely nonexistent. What the programs were actually detecting was normal Internet activity, and many of the false alarms could be prevented by setting up the

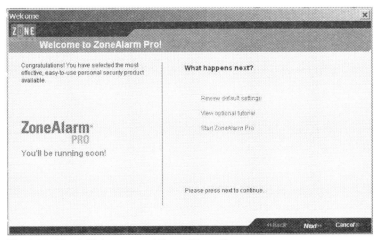

Fig.1.28   The initial screen of Zone Alarm Pro

program to ignore certain programs accessing the Internet. Some of these programs were virtually unusable though.

Modern firewall programs mostly operate in a rather less "in your face" fashion, and produce fewer interruptions. Even so, it is usually necessary to go through a setting up process in order to keep down the number of false alarms, and further tweaking may be needed in order to get things working really well. Of course, if you would like to be informed about every possible attack on the system, most firewalls will duly oblige provided the appropriate settings are used. This certainly gives the ultimate in security, but it could make surfing the Internet a very slow and tedious process.

Zone Alarm

There are plenty of software firewalls to choose from, and most of them are capable of providing your PC with a high degree of security. Black Ice Defender is a popular program that has the advantage of requiring little setting up before it is ready for use. ZoneAlarm is another popular firewall, and it exists in free, trial, and full commercial versions. It is quite easy to set up and use, and the free version represents a good starting point for private users wishing to try a good quality firewall at minimum cost. All versions of this program are reasonably easy to set up.

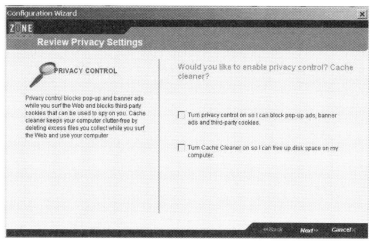

Fig.1.29 Two optional extras are available

ZoneAlarm Pro will be used for this example, and this program has a few more facilities than the basic (free) version.

Figure 1.28 shows the initial window produced once the installation process has been completed. This simply explains that there are a few

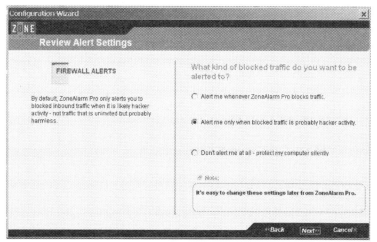

Fig.1.30 Here you select the level of alerts that will be produced

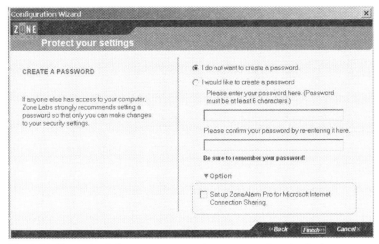

Fig.1.31 If required, the program can be password protected

processes to complete before the program is ready for use. The options available at the next screen (Figure 1.29) are for two of Zone Alarm Pro's optional extras. One of these is a routine that blocks pop-up advertisements and third-party "spy" cookies. Pop-ups are now so widespread on the Internet that they have become a major nuisance. Apart from being irksome, they can slow down your Internet connection by increasing the amount of data that has to be downloaded. This can be a serious drag on your surfing if you do not have some form of broadband connection. A pop-up blocker is therefore a very useful feature.

Cache cleaning is the other option. Copies of many Internet files are kept on a PC so that they do not have to be downloaded again when the relevant pages are revisited. Anyone undertaking a lot of surfing is likely to end up with many megabytes of cached Internet files on their PC's hard disc. These files should eventually be removed by Windows, but the cache cleaner provides a neater solution by preventing a massive build-up from occurring in the first place.

Things then move on to a window (Figure 1.30) where you choose the types of Internet access that will produce alerts. You can opt to have an onscreen message appear when any access is blocked, or for no alerts to be issued. Note that the program will still continue to block Internet access as and when it sees fit, even if the alerts are completely switched

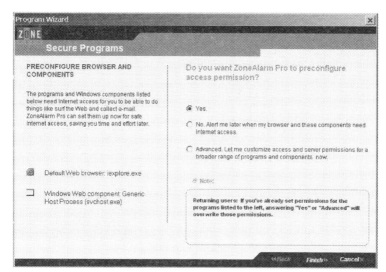

*Fig.1.32 You can choose which programs are granted Internet access
           now or later*

off.   The middle option results in an alert being produced when the
program considers that attempted access is probably the result of an
attack by a hacker.   This is the default option and is probably the best
choice.

The next window (Figure 1.31) enables the program to be password
protected.   This is only necessary if someone else has access to your
PC. This is followed by the screen of Figure 1.32.   Here ZoneAlarm lists
programs that it thinks will need Internet access.   The list will include the
default browser and any other programs that are required for normal
Internet access. By default, these programs will be given Internet access,
but other programs will produce a warning message if they attempt to
use the Internet. Access will then be allowed only if you give permission.
You might prefer to choose which programs will be granted access during
the setting up process rather than dealing with it later as programs try to
access the Internet. As most programs do not require Internet access, it
is probably easier to grant access as and when necessary.

The next window (Figure 1.33) gives the option of starting the program
or viewing a quick tutorial.   It is definitely a good idea to look at the
tutorial, but it can be viewed at any time by running ZoneAlarm Pro and
operating the Tutorial button.

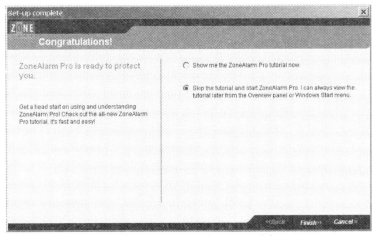

Fig.1.33 You can start the program or view a tutorial

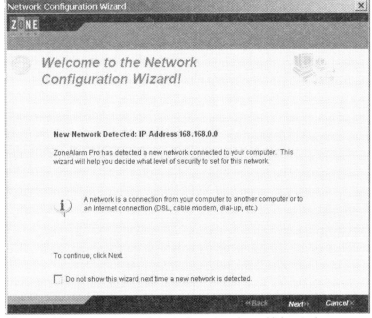

*Fig.1.34 The program has detected a network, and it has to be
configured so that Zone Alarm will permit file sharing*

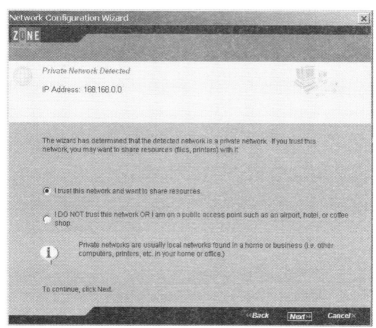

Fig.1.35 The network can be enabled or blocked

Network

The PC used for this demonstration has its Internet connection provided by a broadband modem that has a built-in router, with two other PCs connected to the router. This network was detected by Zone Alarm Pro (Figure 1.34), and the Network Configuration Wizard was launched. Remember that a firewall will block any network access, including the LAN (local area network) variety, unless instructed otherwise. At the next screen (Figure 1.35) you have the option of enabling this network or blocking it. Obviously it must be enabled in order to permit the system to go on working properly.

The window of Figure 1.36 enables the network to be given a name of you choice, or you can simply settle for the default name. The next window (Figure 1.37) simply shows the settings you have chosen and provides an opportunity to go back and changes them. Finally, the program is run (Figure 1.38). In normal use the program runs in the

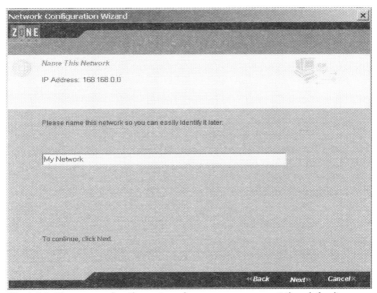

Fig.1.36 Here you give the network a name or accept the default

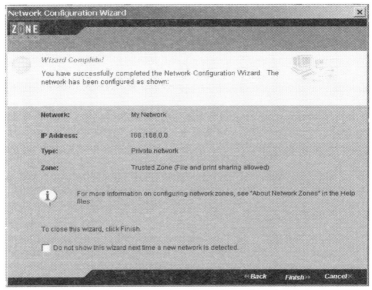

Fig.1.37 Use this window to review the selected settings

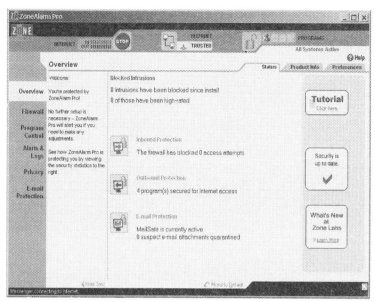

Fig.1.38 Finally, the program is operational

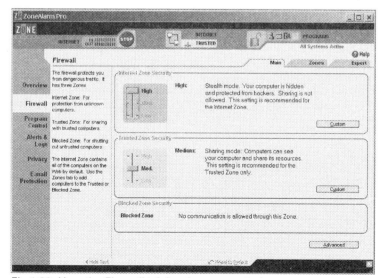

Fig.1.39 Here the Firewall tab has been operated

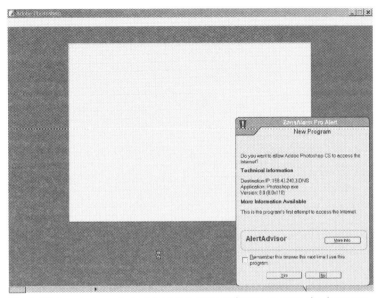

Fig.1.40 An alert produced by a program trying to access the Internet

background and it is only necessary to go to this screen if you need to make changes to the setup or view the statistics produced by the program.

Operating the Firewall tab switches the window to look like Figure 1.39, and the degree of security in each zone can then be adjusted via the slider controls. Unless there is good reason to change the setting for the Internet Zone, it should be left at High. The other tabs permit easy control of other aspects of the program, such as alerts (Figure 1.40). Therefore, if you find any of the initial settings unsatisfactory it is easy to change them.

In use it is likely that the program will initially query potential problems that are really just a normal part of PC's operation. In the example of Figure 1.40 an alert has been triggered by an image editing program trying to access the Internet. Although there is no obvious reason for such a program requiring the Internet, many programs these days use the Internet to regularly look for program updates. Operate the Yes button to permit Internet access or the No button to block it. Tick the checkbox if you would like this answer to be used automatically each time the program tries to access the Internet.

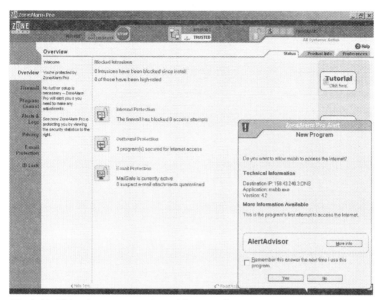

Fig.1.41 This alert was produced by an adware component

Sometimes the alert will genuinely find something that is amiss. In Figure 1.41 the alert shows that a file called msbb.exe has tried to access the Internet. Some delving on the Internet revealed that this is part of the Ncase adware program, which was supposedly uninstalled from the PC a few weeks earlier. Clearly it had not been successfully uninstalled, and some further work was needed in order to banish it from the system.

Internet security can be a bit irksome, and it is something that all of us would probably rather just ignore. Further security measures are needed when wi-fi links are added to a network, and this subject is covered in chapter 4. Unfortunately, security is an issue that no Internet user can afford to ignore these days, and it something that network users really must take seriously.

Points to remember

Over the years many types of interface have been used for networking. These days the only interface commonly used for networking PCs is the Ethernet type, which is also known as a 10/100 network interface. The two figures in the 10/100 name refer to the speeds (in Mbits per second) of the original and current versions of this interface.

Many PCs now have a built-in Ethernet port as standard, but this facility is easily added to a desktop PC. It is just a matter of fitting a PCI Ethernet expansion card. It is also possible to obtain USB Ethernet adapters for use with desktop and portable PCs. Note that a USB 2.0 adapter is needed in order to utilise the full speed of the Ethernet interface.

If you add a PCI Ethernet or wi-fi card to a PC, take the necessary precautions to avoid damaging anything with static charges. A few simple handling precautions are all that is needed to avoid problems.

A network can use wi-fi for every link, but this is unlikely to be the most practical solution. For short links a wired connection using Ethernet ports will cost less, provide faster transfers, and give better security.

The most basic network consists of two PCs linked via their Ethernet ports. This requires a "crossed" cable and not the more usual "straight" type. In order to network more than two computers it is necessary to have a router, with the Ethernet port of each PC connected to the router by way of a "straight" cable.

It is not necessary to buy any software in order to implement a basic but useful network. The built-in networking facilities of Windows permit files, folders, or even complete discs to be shared. It is also possible to for a printer connected to one PC to be used by other PCs in the network.

Some printers can be connected direct to the network and used by any PC in the system. This facility is not available using low-cost printers, but it is sometimes available as an option. Any printer can converted into a network type by using it with a device called a "printer server".

It is possible to share the Internet connection of one PC via the network. In practice this is not a very good way of doing things though. If the PC that has the Internet connection is switched off, all the other PCs in the network lose their Internet connection. The PC connected to the modem acts as a kind of router, and this can be a significant drain on its resources.

Using a broadband modem connected to a router (or a single unit that combines both functions) provides an always-on Internet connection for every PC in the network. It does so without increasing the workload of any PC in the system, and need not cost very much.

Antivirus programs are of limited use against hackers. In order to keep hackers at bay it is essential to use either or software or hardware firewall. Ideally, both should be used if you have some form of broadband connection, especially if it is of the "always on" variety.

1 Networking basics

Going wi-fi

Why wireless?

Back in the early days of radio it was apparently quite common for a non-technical person on seeing all the wires inside a set to ask why it was called a "wireless". A wireless network lives up to its name rather better than the early radio sets. There might be a short lead from the back of a PC to a box of electronics on the top, but many wi-fi setups have no wiring worth mentioning. For many users this is really the only advantage of the wi-fi approach, but for most it is a major plus point. A short lead from a computer to a router or other piece of networking equipment is not difficult to implement, particularly if the two pieces of equipment are on the same desk. No do-it-yourself skills are likely to be required.

The situation is very different when the items to be linked are on opposite sides of the room. An "off the shelf" lead is all that is needed to connect the two pieces of equipment, but keeping the lead tucked away discretely out of sight is more difficult. This is not just a matter of making things look pretty, and there is the safety aspect to consider. A lead placed where people keep tripping over is obviously unsafe, although in practice it is probably the networking equipment that is most likely to suffer. It becomes increasing difficult to keep things neat and safe as more equipment is added to the network. A certain amount of do-it-yourself ability is needed in order to install the wiring properly, but it is not too difficult to make a good job of it.

Installing the wiring becomes much more difficult when leads have to be run from one room to another. This type of thing is still within the abilities of the average handyman with an electric drill, but it is not everyone's "cup of tea". Also, it is not a practical proposition unless you are prepared to have holes for the cables drilled in the walls, floors, and ceilings. Apart from aesthetic considerations, having a house entwined with various networking cables could adversely affect its resale value. In the case of a listed building, it is unlikely that permission to install the wiring would be obtained.

It is usually possible to use ready-made cables, but this could mean having to use some standard lengths that are substantially longer than you require. You then have to hide a few metres of cable safely out of the way where no one will trip over it. The bits and pieces needed to make your own custom cables are readily available, but this is a more difficult approach. Surprisingly perhaps, making your own cables can be relatively expensive when all the costs are taken into account.

Drawbacks

Having the longer links provided by wi-fi equipment has a huge advantage for most network users, but there are a few disadvantages to take into account when considering the wi-fi option. The obvious one is the higher cost, although as technology becomes cheaper this becomes a less significant drawback. At the time of writing this book the additional cost is still significant, although for slower wi-fi equipment it is becoming much less of an issue. It is a matter of pricing the various options and making your own subjective assessment with the prices prevailing at the time. With a typical home or small business network there will often be just one or two links that could really benefit from a wireless connection, which should help to keep the additional cost well within reason.

The relatively slow speed of wireless systems is another potential drawback. Although a wired network has a notional speed of 10 or 100 megabits per second, in the real world any equipment you use will support the higher rate. A modern Ethernet system therefore works at 100 megabits per second and you can forget the lower rate. You will never use it. Wi-fi systems normally operate at 11 or 54 megabits per second.

In practice, even a transfer rate of 11 megabits per second could be perfectly adequate. For many users, the point of networking a system is to share a broadband Internet connection. A standard ADSL connection operates with a download rate of 512 kilobits (0.512 megabits) per second, with an upload rate of just half that figure. Even allowing for inefficiencies in the systems, both types of wi-fi link can easily handle the sharing of an ADSL broadband Internet connection. Some broadband connections operate at higher rates of one or two megabits per second, but this is still well within the capabilities of wi-fi equipment.

Wi-fi connections are also perfectly adequate for some types of file sharing. It is popular to use a home network to permit music files stored on one computer to be played on another PC in the system. Music files generally operate at about 64 to 256 kilobits per second, with a few operating at up to about 512k per second. This is again well within the capabilities of a wi-fi connection. Many of the videos played on PCs use a similar bit rate, but high quality video requires higher rates that could stretch a wi-fi system. This is not of significance to most home and small business users though.

The speed of a wi-fi system is likely to be sluggish when transferring large files or large numbers of files from one PC to another. In theory it is possible for a system operating at 11 megabits per second to transfer more than one megabyte of data a second, but in practice the transfer rate could be little more than half this rate. To transfer 500 megabytes of data would therefore take at least eight minutes, and could well take closer to 15 minutes. For this type of thing transfers at 54 megabits per second are preferable, enabling 500 megabytes of data to be transferred in around one and a half to three minutes. A wired network would complete the task in little more than half the time, but would still be something less than instant.

Range

Although, on the face of it, a wi-fi link is more than adequate for most users, there is a "fly in the ointment" that should not be overlooked. The quoted speeds for wi-fi equipment are the highest that can be achieved, and they require quite strong signal levels. Do not be misled by the ranges quoted for wi-fi equipment, which are often something like 100 metres, and in some cases much higher figures are quoted. A useable signal may be obtained at a range as large as 100 metres, but only with clear air between the aerials. Where longer ranges are quoted, these are usually for operation at speeds well below the maximum transfer rate.

When using a wi-fi link from one room to another there will inevitably be walls, floors, ceilings, and all-manner of obstructions between the aerials. How much (or little) effect these have on the signal strength is not totally predictable, and the only way to find out is to use a "suck it and see" approach. Buildings that have large amounts of metal in their structure can be problematic, but a reasonable operating range should otherwise be obtained. A range of 10 or 20 metres is usually possible, but at longer ranges the transfer rate is likely to be significantly less than notional 11 or 54 megabits per second.

When reduced speed is obtained, results should still be adequate for sharing a broadband Internet connection, audio files, etc., but a wired network would probably be a better choice for transferring large amounts of data. An unfortunate truism is that wi-fi equipment performs the worst in situations where it would be by far the most convenient solution. With a large distance plus walls and floors between the two units to be linked, using a connecting cable is very difficult. In this situation a wi-fi link is a much easier option that avoids the awkward wiring, but getting a strong signal is likely to prove difficult. In practice it is likely that many users will be prepared to put up with reduced speed in order to avoid the inconveniences of installing wiring.

Security

Computer security has become a major issue in recent years. There seems to be a significant number of criminals continually thinking up new scams or finding ways of reworking old ones. The early viruses were produced by individuals who were really just showing off, and trying to show how clever they were. It has now become rather more sinister, with people trying to find ways of extracting money from companies or private individuals using what we now know as cyber crime. All Internet users now have to take security very seriously, but it is particularly important to the growing band of users that have a broadband connection.

You do not have to be a computer genius to see that using wi-fi links has the potential to let hackers "eavesdrop" on your network or even gain access to it. At the most basic level, anyone operating a wi-fi equipped PC within the range of your system could have free Internet access by way of your network and Internet connection. This would probably not matter a great deal if you have an unlimited broadband connection. The unwanted guest would effectively reduce the bandwidth of the Internet connection, but probably not to a significant degree.

Someone using your Internet connection could prove costly if you have capped access, where extra has to be paid if more than a certain amount is downloaded each month. Either way, are you really unconcerned about others gaining access to your network for a bit of freeloading? Most of us value our privacy and would prefer to keep the network totally closed to outsiders, even if they have no really sinister intent.

Of course, some hackers trying to enter the network might have a sinister motive. With no security measures in use, someone could potentially hack into your network and gain personal information stored on the system, or even steal passwords or other sensitive information. Unless the network is used for purely unimportant applications such as games or entertainment, it is essential to take steps to keep it secure. Even if the system is only used for trivia, you would presumably still prefer not to have strangers using your Internet connection and accessing your PC.

Security is covered in chapter 5, but it is worth making the point here that much wi-fi equipment will install very easily. Indeed, in some cases it requires no setup information at all from the user. However, equipment of this type is installed without any of the built-in security measures being implemented. There is a temptation to simply "let well alone", and not bother with implementing the security measures. With the network working well, why risk messing up the installation? Taking this attitude is definitely a mistake though, and it is a good idea to read the instruction manuals and get everything set up properly as soon as possible. Setting up a network to make it secure is quite simple and does not take long.

Interference

The range of frequencies available for use with wi-fi networks is quite narrow, but the allocation is broad enough to permit a number of channels to be accommodated. As will be explained later, there are actually two bands available for this type of equipment, and these are at frequencies near 2.4GHz and 5GHz. At present the vast majority of wi-fi devices operate in the 2.4GHz band, and this book is primarily about this type of wi-fi equipment.

Even though there are several channels, congestion is still a potential problem. This depends on where you live, and to some extent it is a matter of luck. I live in a part of the country that has quite a high population density, but my home wi-fi network has yet to detect any other users. Although the short range of this equipment is normally considered to be a drawback, in this context it is definitely an advantage. In fact a range of a few miles would render wi-fi networks unusable as in many areas interference from other networks would render most systems useless.

The short operating range largely avoids this problem in suburban and rural areas, but if you operate a wi-fi network in a town it is quite likely that you will find that you are not alone. Switching away from the default channel should avoid any major problems with interference from other systems. As wi-fi becomes more popular it could be difficult to find a totally clear channel in heavily built-up areas, giving a more limited operating range. Also, bear in mind that having several systems nearby could reduce the range somewhat even if they are not operating on the same channel as your system.

Many wi-fi users are probably under the impression that a band has been set aside specifically for wireless networking. Unfortunately, this is not the case, and wi-fi shares the 2.4GHz band with several other types of equipment. These include such things as some cordless phone systems, baby monitors, Bluetooth devices, video senders, cordless headphones, and even microwave ovens. These devices all add to the congestion, and can potentially block some channels completely. They also add to the general noise on the band and tend to limit the maximum operating range. Again, in suburban and rural areas any problems should be minimal, but performance could be seriously compromised in some parts of towns.

Hotspots

The lack of wires to connect the system together is the main reason for using a wi-fi setup, but it does have one or two additional advantages that should not be overlooked. If the system includes any laptop or other portable computers it would be normal to equip each of them with some form of wi-fi adapter. Apart from avoiding the need to fiddle with wires each time a portable devices is connected to or removed from the network, a wi-fi connection makes it possible to access the network from just about anywhere in the building. In fact it should be possible to connect to the network from the garden, or possibly even the shed or summerhouse at the bottom of the garden. You can therefore surf the Internet while outside in the garden on a fine summer evening.

In order to access the Internet it is not even necessary to return home, since wireless hotspots offer Internet access in numerous locations around the world. A wireless hotspot is a wireless access point (WAP) that connects to some form of Internet service. This will typically be a 512k ADSL broadband connection, but it could be some other type of broadband service. It should certainly be something much faster than an ordinary dialup connection, but bear in mind that you might have to share the service with other users, which could noticeably slow things down.

The idea is to have hotspots in restaurants, cafes, motorway service stations, hotels, trains, airports, or anywhere convenient for potential users. As one would expect, these services are not usually free, and the hourly connection rates are quite high. Even so, this method can be cost-effective for those requiring Internet access on the move. The speed of the connection is also likely to be much faster than the alternatives, which are unlikely to be significantly cheaper. Some hotspots are provided free of charge, so you might get lucky from time to time and obtain free Internet access.

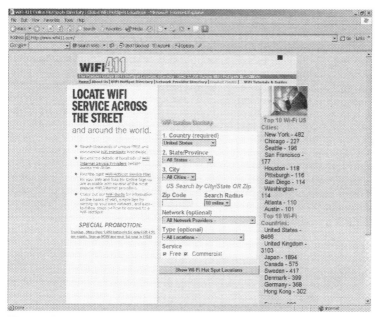

Fig.2.1   The default is for a search of the United States

Hotspots are aptly named, and due to their very limited area of coverage it is important to be in the right place in order to access one. Simply being in the right general area is unlikely to be good enough. The number of hotspots is increasing all the time, and at the time of writing this there are well over one thousand of them in the London area. Even so, it is a good idea to locate potential hotspots before setting out on a journey. There is a very useful site at this address:

www.wifi411.com

It defaults to a search of the United States (Figure 2.1), but the menu near the top of the page enables the UK to be selected. Then the search can be refined further by using the other menus to select the appropriate part of the UK, and then a town within that area. It is also possible to select a particular network provider and a type of location (hotel, bus station, etc.). The checkboxes enable the search to be limited to either

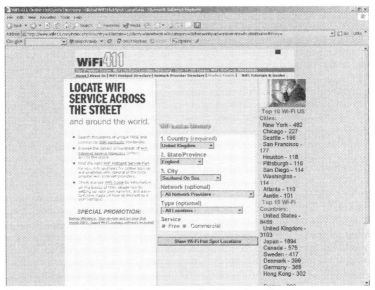

Fig.2.2 A search has been set up for Southend on Sea

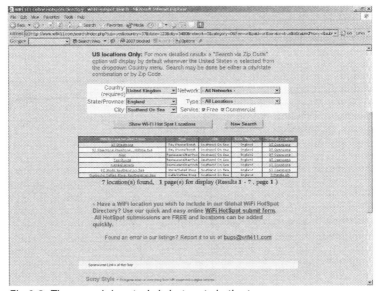

Fig.2.3 The search located six hotspots in the town

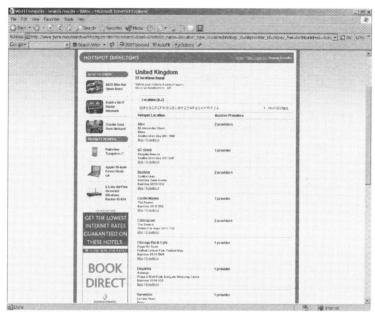

*Fig.2.4 Some 22 results have been produced for the general
Southend on Sea area*

free or commercial access points, but the number of free services is so
small that it is probably pointless to search for them alone.

A search for any access points in Southend on Sea (Figure 2.2) produced
six results (Figure 2.3), with no less than five of these being part of the
BT Openzone network. Four sites in the list are at cafes and restaurants,
two are at payphones, and one is at a store owned by a well-known
computer chain. The train and bus stations are conspicuously absent
from the list, and as yet neither of these seem to be used much for wireless
hotspots in the UK.

There are other hotspot search engines, and these two are well worth
trying:

www.jiwire.com

www.hotspot-hotel.com

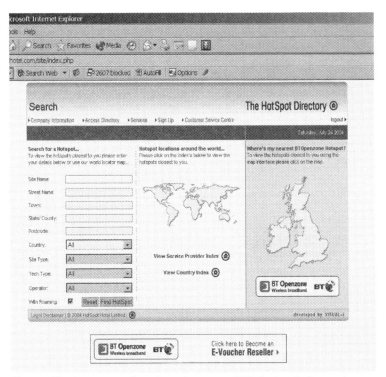

Fig.2.5 You have to register in order to use BT's hotspot site

The first of these is owned by Intel, and using it to search for hotspots in the Southend on Sea area produced an impressive 22 results (Figure 2.4). However, it actually searched a much wider area than the wifi411 search engine, and most of the sites listed were actually in nearby towns. The second site is owned by BT, and it is necessary to go through a free registration process in order to reach the search engine (Figure 2.5).

A conventional search engine is available in the left-hand section of the window, or you can use the maps to the right of this. Left-clicking the UK map first produces a larger map of the UK (Figure 2.6), and left-clicking on this produces a large-scale map of the selected area (Figure 2.7). It is then possible to obtain a scrollable street plan of that area (Figure 2.8) so that the locations of hotspots can be precisely identified. A list of the hotspots together with addresses is provided beneath the street plan.

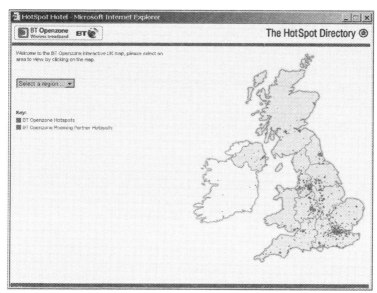

Fig.2.6 Left-clicking the UK map produces this larger version

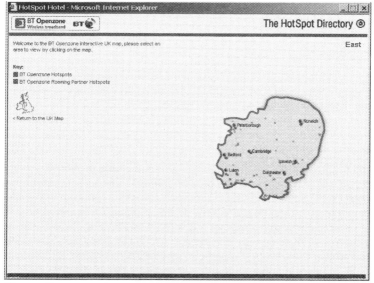

Fig.2.7 You next select the region of interest

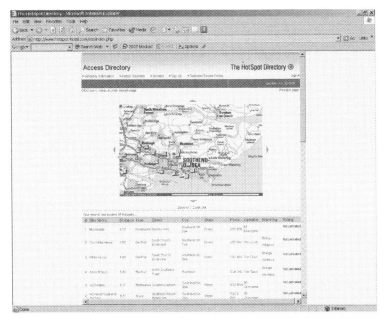

Fig.2.8 A scrollable street map shows the hotspots, which are also
listed in the area beneath the map

Roaming

You will probably encounter the term "roaming" when dealing with
wireless hotspots. This can simply be a reference to the fact that you
can literally roam with your laptop and still stay connected to the Internet,
but remember that you can not roam far. At best you can only be about
100 metres from the hotspot's aerial, and the maximum range could well
be much less than that.

More normally, this term refers to agreements between rival service
providers that permit users of one service to go online using the
equipment of another hotspot provider. Given the patchy coverage at
present, this type of thing can make life much easier for users. However,
the added convenience of roaming is likely to cost extra, where it is an
option at all. At some locations it is possible to gain instant access to the
hotspot by purchasing a voucher over-the-counter at the location. In
other cases it is possible to sign up and pay online using a credit or
debit card.

Standards

Computer standards have tended to be something of a joke in the past. Standards have not only been a problem in the world of computing. The electronics industry in general has experienced problems with competing standards, which inevitably results in many people buying gadgets that soon become obsolete. In fact competing standards can ultimately kill the product, producing a situation where there are no winners and plenty of losers.

An additional problem with computer standards is that manufacturers have tended to "do their own thing" rather than rigidly adhering to agreed standards. It is difficult to understand why a manufacturer would release a product that does not strictly adhere to the rules, but this was quite common in the past. Possibly it was the result of cost cutting, or perhaps it was just poor design work that was to blame. Anyway, even something as basic as trying to get a printer to work properly with a serial or parallel port used to be very difficult. Although "off the shelf" leads were usually available, ready-made leads often proved to be inadequate.

Fortunately, the situation has improved somewhat over the years, and wi-fi is certainly free from many of the problems associated with wired interfaces. Inevitably though, there is more than one standard to contend with. The wireless networking equipment in common use conforms to the standards laid down by the Institute of Electrical and Electronics Engineers, or the IEEE as it is more commonly called. All the wi-fi equipment falls within the 802.11 standard, but there are three versions of it (802.11a, 802.11b, and 802.11g). Table 1 summarises the important differences between the three 802.11 standards.

The ranges quoted here are theoretical, and would probably not be obtained in practice. These are the maximum ranges at the maximum operating speed, and longer ranges can be achieved at lower speeds. Bear in mind that ranges quoted for operation outdoors assume that there is clear air between the aerials. Walls, fences, and other solid objects between the aerials, particularly if they are made from metal, will substantially reduce the range.

I tried operating a 802.11b link between two systems about 100 metres apart, hoping that there would be a sufficiently strong signal to permit one system to use the broadband Internet connection of the other. In practice the two systems remained oblivious to each other, with neither system picking up a discernable signal from the other. There were a few trees and other obstructions between the two aerials, and that was sufficient to shield each aerial from the other unit's signal. The only way

Table 1

Standard	802.11a	802.11b	802.11g
Maximum speed	54Mbits/s	11Mbits/s	54Mbits/s
Real-world speed	20Mbits/s	4.5Mbits/s	20Mbits/s
Range (outdoors)	30 metres	120 metres	50 metres
Range (indoors)	12 metres	60 metres	20 metres
Band	5GHz	2.4GHz	2.4GHz
Users	64	32	32
Total UK channels	8	13	13
Separate channels	8	3	3
Compatibility	-	802.11g	802.11b
Wi-fi certified	Yes	Yes	Yes

to find the maximum usable operating range is to try it and see, but slightly pessimistic forecasts are usually the most accurate.

As already explained, the maximum range indoors is heavily dependent on the type and number of obstructions between the two aerials. A couple of plasterboard walls are unlikely to have much effect on the range, but a few substantial brick walls could massively reduce it. A large metal radiator in the wrong place could totally block the signal. In difficult surroundings, 802.11b equipment probably offers the greatest chance of providing useable results.

5GHz band

802.11a equipment has the advantage of not operating in the overused 2.4GHz band, and it also permits twice as many users per access point. However, for a home or small business network it is unlike that more than 32 users will need to use an access point. There are some drawbacks to 802.11a equipment, and probably the most important one for most potential users is that the cost is much higher than for equivalent 802.11b and 802.11g equipment.

The economics of networking are at least as capricious as those for other aspects of computing, but at the time of writing this, opting for 802.11a equipment means paying more than twice as much for the privilege. Another important factor to bear in mind is that there is relatively little 802.11a equipment available, although choice and availability should improve in due course. Because 802.11a equipment operates on a different band, it is totally incompatible with the other two standards. 802.11b and 802.11g equipment can be freely mixed, but transfers will obviously be at the lower rate if one unit in a link is of the 802.11b variety.

Note that it is possible to obtain 802.11a equipment that is compatible with the other two standards. However, this compatibility is presumably obtained by combining 802.11a and 802.11g gadgets in a single box. As one would expect, the extra hardware required tends to make these units relatively expensive. They are extremely versatile though.

Channels

On the face of it, the 802.11a standard provides fewer channels than the other two standards. In reality it is actually better, since its eight channels do not overlap, and they are genuine channels. The 13 channels of the other two systems overlap to some extent, so significant interference between units operating on adjacent channels is quite possible. In fact the channel overlap problem is so great that it is only possible to have three totally separate channels. Together with its operation on the 5GHz band, this makes 802.11a equipment a safer choice in areas where there is severe congestion.

Wi-fi Alliance

In theory, equipment manufactured to conform to one of the three IEEE standards should work perfectly with any other equipment designed to meet the same standard (or a compatible one). In reality it is never as simple as this with such complex technology, and there have been incompatibility issues in the past. In some cases the level of performance obtained was below expectations, and in extreme cases no useable link was obtained.

The Wi-fi Alliance was formed in 1999, and its purpose was to certify that wi-fi equipment fully conformed to the appropriate standard and would operate properly with any equipment of the same or a compatible standard. A certified 802.11g access point should therefore operate perfectly with any certified 802.11b or 802.11g wireless adapter. Wi-fi certified equipment carries the Wi-fi logo, and it should also have a badge of approval (Figure 2.9). The badge shows which standard or standards

Fig.2.9 A typical certification badge

the equipment is compatible with, and it also indicates whether it has protected access. In other words, it shows whether the equipment has built-in security measures to keep unauthorised users out of the system.

Is it essential to obtain equipment that has wi-fi certification? In theory it is safer to do so, but the fact that a unit lacks certification does not necessarily mean that it lacks full compatibility with the relevant standard. In fact, such equipment is likely to be perfectly usable. The wi-fi badge of approval is not as common as one might expect, and there is plenty of good quality equipment available that does not sport the wi-fi logo. On checking a mixture of "big name" and generic wi-fi units I found that very few had the badge of approval.

The cost of gaining approval has certainly deterred some manufacturers from seeking certification for their products. Added costs are obviously unwelcome when making any products, but they are particularly unhelpful when producing cheap generic devices. There is little chance of obtaining approved products if you take the cheap generic route, and customer support is often poor or nonexistent with these units. On the plus side, generic products are almost certain to be based on exactly the same chips as equivalents from the well-known companies.

For those with limited experience of dealing with computer hardware it is probably better to opt for equipment from one of the well-known manufacturers such as Netgear, Belkin, US Robotics, and 3Com. If the equipment is from a respected company and it also has certification, so much the better. If it does not have certification, at least there should be a proper customer support service to get things sorted out, and you are protected by your statutory rights.

Bluetooth

There is a common misconception that Bluetooth and wi-fi equipment are the same, or that they are to some extent compatible. The confusion is perhaps understandable, since Bluetooth equipment uses the same 2.4GHz band as most wireless networking equipment, and its function is much the same. It provides a wireless link between two pieces of electronic equipment. Despite the superficial similarities, the purpose of Bluetooth is very different to that of wi-fi equipment.

Wi-fi is an extension of the Ethernet networking system, and when using wi-fi equipment you have what is essentially an Ethernet based network. A typical wi-fi network will include some wired connections using standard Ethernet

Fig.2.10 Bluetooth is used for a wide range of products, including headsets

ports and cables. Bluetooth is not intended for networking, although it could probably be used to provide networking. Using Bluetooth equipment in this fashion would be doing things the hard way though, and wi-fi equipment performs this task much more efficiently.

The real purpose of Bluetooth is to link two devices, and it is a general-purpose system which is designed to accommodate practically any two pieces of equipment that could be usefully linked. Bluetooth is used for such things as connecting a computer to a printer, a laptop PC to a desktop computer, and a notebook PC to a mobile phone. It can even be used for a non-digital application such as cordless headphones and hands-free headsets (Figure 2.10).

Wireless links have been used with PCs for many years in the form of IrDA infrared links. The main problem with the infra-red approach was that it was basically just a short range line of sight system, although for many purposes this was perfectly adequate. When uploading from a digital camera or a laptop computer to a PC for example, the two devices would probably be more or less side-by-side anyway. Another limitation of IrDA is that it is based on a standard serial port, and it has the relatively low bit rates associated with this type of port. The maximum transfer rate is usually about 115kbits (0.115Mbits) per second, and in some cases is much less than this.

Bluetooth is designed to be a sort of universal version of an IrDA link, with a higher level of performance. It is designed to operate with low levels of power consumption, making it suitable for use with small portable devices such as phones and palmtop PCs. With a maximum transfer speed of only about 1Mbit per second, Bluetooth is not particularly fast by modern computing standards. It is only about one tenth as fast as an 802.11b link for instance. The transfer speed is adequate for many purposes though, and it is nearly ten times faster than an IrDA link.

The range of a Bluetooth device is about 10 metres, and because it uses a radio link rather than infrared, the signal is able to pass through many types of object. It can be blocked by large pieces of metal though. It is possible to obtain signal repeaters that can boost the range to 100 metres, but Bluetooth is normally used in applications where a range of 10 metres is adequate.

Although Bluetooth devices have a very short operating range, they still need security measures in order to keep hackers at bay. Security measures are built into the system, and Bluetooth gadgets have unique identifying codes that can be used to prevent any unauthorised use. For instance, a Bluetooth mobile phone could be set up so that it would only connect to the Internet when used with your own Pocket PC.

Piconet

When Bluetooth devices lock-on to each others' signals they form what is termed a piconet, or a small network in other words. One gadget initiates contact, and this is the master device. This unit negotiates all data transfer paths between devices in the network, and there can be up to seven slave units in addition to the master. In practice it is unlikely that eight units would be networked using Bluetooth, and in most cases it is used with just two devices. However, it could be used in a situation such as a Bluetooth enabled printer being fed from several PCs.

Any Bluetooth device has the wherewithal to control a piconet, and the master – slave relationship has to be flexible so that the equipment can adjust to suit practically any situation. With a simple swap of data between two devices, the one that initiates the connection becomes the master device. Any other units that join the piconet will automatically operate as slaves.

This simple scheme of things does not suit all situations, and it would not work in the printer setup mentioned previously. The first computer to access the printer would become the master unit, but for this network to operate properly it is necessary for the printer to always be the master device. This enables the printer to properly control the flow of print jobs. The way around this is for a master device to be temporarily demoted to slave status when it links with a device that must have master status.

Channels

Bluetooth uses the same 2.4GHz band as 802.11b and 802.11g wi-fi units, but the channelling is arranged differently. The lower bit rate of Bluetooth permits a larger number of channels to be accommodated, and there are some 79 separate channels. There is no need to select a channel, since a system of channel hopping is used. Devices "hop" 1600 times a second in an attempt to avoid conflicts.

The system used with Bluetooth is called Adaptive Frequency Hopping (AFH), and it is designed to avoid interference from any devices that use the 2.4GHz band, and not just other Bluetooth equipment. As signals within the band come and go, Bluetooth devices will adapt to the changing situation in an attempt to make the best possible use of any free channels.

Bluetooth had quite a long gestation period, and when first launched its level of take-up was somewhat underwhelming. It is backed by the Bluetooth Special Interest Group (www.bluetooth.com), which has over 2000 members including huge companies such as Intel and IBM. It is gaining in popularity, but has yet to achieve its creators' aim of becoming a worldwide standard for short-range communications without cables. It seems likely that it will do so in due course.

Incidentally, Bluetooth is named after a Harold Bluetooth Gormson. He is not one of the brains behind the system, but was in fact the monarch of Demark just over a thousand years ago. Apparently, he managed the difficult task of uniting two Baltic states, which seems to a rather tenuous link to modern wireless technology.

Points to remember

The main advantage of wireless networking is the obvious one of avoiding the need to thread cables around the house or office. This is a huge advantage for a home system where unsightly cables are deemed to be unacceptable, or where adding cables is simply not allowed for some reason.

The ranges quoted for wi-fi systems have to be taken with the proverbial "pinch of salt". The quoted ranges might be achieved in practice, but typical operating ranges seem to be somewhat less than the specifications would suggest. Operation is still possible with low signal strengths, but not at anything like the full quoted transfer rate.

Inefficiencies in the system mean that data can not be transferred at the quoted rates. In practice it is likely that the actual rate will be a little under half the quoted figure. Note also that the rates are in bits per second, not bytes per second. Divide speed figures by eight in order to obtain a transfer rate in bytes per second.

There is only one standard for wi-fi equipment, which is the IEEE 802.11 standard. However, matters are complicated by having three different versions of it (802.11a, 802.11b, and 802.11g). While the 802.11a equipment has potential advantages, it relatively expensive, difficult to obtain, and is incompatible with the other two.

It is 802.11b and 802.11g equipment that are used in most home and small office wi-fi systems. The faster 802.11g equipment is compatible with the 802.11b variety, but when a link uses the two types of equipment it obviously operates at the slower rate.

Bear in mind that it might be easy to set up a wireless network by simply accepting the defaults, but doing so will almost certainly leave the system wide open to hackers. Modern wi-fi equipment has built-in security measures, and it is import to protect your system by ensuring that these are properly set up.

The short operating range helps to avoid problems with interference due to there being too many wi-fi users in the vicinity, but it is still a potential problem in heavily built-up areas. The problem is worse with 802.11b and 802.11g equipment which has fewer non-overlapping channels, and shares the 2.4GHz band with other types of equipment.

A wi-fi equipped laptop or notebook PC can be used to access wireless hotspots at cafes, libraries, computer shops, etc. With a few exceptions, use of wireless hotspots is not free though. The cost of access can be quite high, but the same is true of the alternatives. The download speed when using hotspots is usually quite, and is typical via a 512k or 1024k ADSL Internet connection.

Many wi-fi equipment manufacturers now have their devices approved by the Wi-fi Alliance, but some do not bother. It is obviously reassuring to have approved equipment in your wireless network, but gadgets from any of the large manufacturers should have full compatibility with the relevant standards. As always, cheap generic equipment is a bit more risky and often lacks worthwhile customer support.

Bluetooth is not used for true networking, and is not really an alternative to 802.11 wi-fi equipment. It can be used for something like wireless printer sharing, but in most cases it is only used to provide a link between two devices such as a notebook PC and a mobile phone. It has a relatively low maximum data transfer rate of 1 Mbits per second, but this is adequate for many tasks.

Practical wi-fi

Getting connected

Any computer that will be connected to the network via a wireless link must be equipped with a wi-fi adapter of some kind. The available options depend on the type of PC, but for a desktop type the main options are a USB wireless adapter or a PCI type. Provided a spare USB port is available, the USB option is the easier to install. Some of these units are similar in appearance to the popular USB pen drives that contain flash memory, and a few of these devices do actually combine the two functions of wi-fi adapter and pen drive. The example shown in Figure 3.1 is purely a wi-fi adapter, which is the more usual approach. There is normally no outward sign of an aerial with these units, as it is contained within the plastic case.

Fig.3.1 A Surecom 802.11b USB adapter

*Fig.3.2 Using a USB extension cable enables the position of a USB
         wi-fi adapter to be adjusted easily*

The adapter can be plugged straight into a USB port of the PC, or
connected via a USB extension lead. Using any unit of this type directly
plugged into a USB port is convenient, but it leaves the device vulnerable
to damage. The risks are probably greater when the device is used with
a heavy desktop PC. If someone should happen to knock against the
adapter it is possible that the PC will remain in place and that the adapter
will give way. This would probably render it unusable, and repairs are
usually uneconomic with low-cost units such as these adapters.

I prefer to use a short extension cable with any small USB gadgets. In
the current context this method has the added advantage of permitting
the adapter to be moved slightly, which can be useful if a "blind" spot is
giving problems with poor performance. Note that it is not a normal A to
B USB cable that is required, but an A to A extension lead. This has the
larger A type socket at one end and an A type plug at the other (Figure
3.2).

USB wi-fi adapters are also available in the form of a small box that sits
on top of the PC and connects to the USB port via a short cable. Figure
3.3 shows a neat unit of this type made by Netgear. This type of adapter
is connected to the USB port via a standard A to B cable, and the rear of

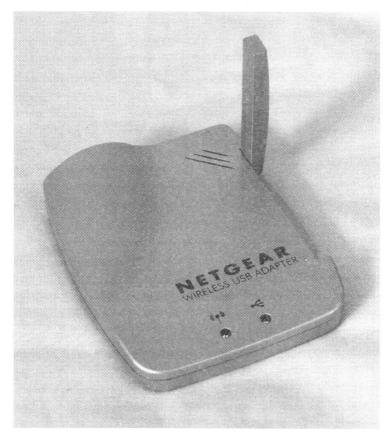

Fig.3.3 This Netgear adapter connects to the PC using an ordinary
(A to B) USB cable

the unit has the smaller B type USB connector (Figure 3.4). This is the
type of cable this is used with scanners, printers, and most other USB
gadgets, but a suitable lead is normally supplied with the adapter.

This style of wireless network adapter tends to be more expensive than
the type that is designed to plug straight into a USB port, but one reason
for this is that many of them are 802.11g devices. The cheap "pen drive"
adapters are 802.11b devices. An advantage of the box and lead style
adapters is that, as standard, the box part can be easily repositioned in
order to find the position that gives optimum results. This is a definite
advantage for an adapter that will be used with a desktop PC, but the

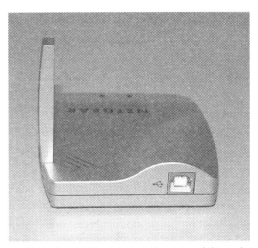

Fig.3.4 The USB socket on the rear of the unit

pen drive type units are probably a better choice for use with portable PCs.

Speed

802.11b adapters usually have a USB 1.1 port, but they will work perfectly well with USB 2.0 ports. On the face of it, a USB 1.1 port is adequate for an 802.11b adapter, since it operates at more or less the same maximum speed as the adapter. In practice it is not quite as simple as that, because USB 1.1 only permits a single device to use half of the available bandwidth. This ensures that one device can not hog all the bandwidth to the detriment of the others. Unfortunately, it also means that USB 1.1 wi-fi adapters might not operate quite as fast as expected, although any shortfall is likely to be quite small.

There is little point in using USB 1.1 for an 802.11g adapter, because the speed of the USB port would be far too low to accommodate the transfer rates possible with the adapter. It is possible to use an 802.11g adapter with a USB 1.1 port if that is all that is available, but data transfers will be limited by the relative slowness of the USB port. USB 2.0 can handle bit rates well above the 54Mbits per second of the 802.11g standard. In fact USB 2.0 can handle rates of up to 480Mbits per second. An 802.11g USB adapter should therefore be capable of operating at full speed with a USB 2.0 port.

Note that it is possible to add USB 2.0 ports to a desktop PC that is only equipped with USB 1.1 ports. It is just a matter of adding a PCI expansion card that is has what will typically be two or four USB 2.0 ports. The generic card shown in Figure 3.5 has four ports and costs only a few pounds. Of course, the PC must have at least one spare PCI expansion slot, but this will not be a problem with most PCs. Windows XP is designed to operate with USB 2.0 ports, but Windows ME is not. However, provided

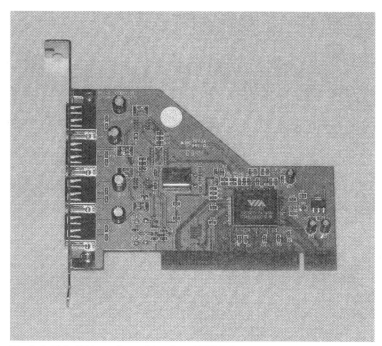

Fig.3.5 This PCI card provides four USB 2.0 ports

you are careful to obtain a card that is supplied with drivers for Windows ME, it should work perfectly well with this operating system.

Hubs

Many PC users augment the two built-in USB ports of their PCs using a PC hub, such as the unit shown in Figure 3.6. This plugs into one of the existing USB ports and effectively splits it to provide extra ports. The hub shown in Figure 3.6 has four ports, but taking into account the port on the PC that it occupies, it provides only three extra ports. A simple hub of this type works well with many devices, but it is less than ideal for gadgets that obtain their power from the USB port. By splitting a single port into three or four ports, the amount of power available from each of these ports is reduced.

Fig.3.6 This passive USB 1.1 hub has four ports

Particularly with USB 1.1 ports, which can supply less power than the USB 2.0 variety, this can result in devices failing to work when used with a simple hub. On plugging in the device, Windows responds with an apologetic message explaining that the hub can not provide sufficient current to power the device you have just connected. 802.11 adapters are not low-power devices, and will probably fail to work if connected via a hub.

The easiest solution is to use a powered hub, which has its own mains power supply unit and does not draw any power from the PC's USB port. A unit of this type should be able to supply the full quota of power to each of its USB ports, and it enables USB devices to be used without increasing the drain on the PC's power supply. The main problem with a powered hub is that you have the hub itself, plus what is invariably an external mains power supply unit to power it. With two extra boxes and a lot of wiring, it is not a particularly neat solution. Where possible, it is better to provide extra USB ports using a PCI expansion card.

A USB 1.1 hub will normally work with a USB 2.0 port, but the additional ports are of the slower USB 1.1 variety. In effect, you a converting one

Fig.3.7 A PCI w-fi adapter complete with aerial

fast USB port into several slower ones. This might suit your requirements, but it is better to leave you options open by using a USB 2.0 hub with a USB 2.0 port. A USB 2.0 hub will normally work with a USB 1.1 port, but it will only provide USB 1.1 ports.

PCI adapter

In some ways a wi-fi PCI card (Figure 3.7) is a neater solution than using any form of USB wi-fi adapter. Apart from the aerial, everything is kept within the main housing of the PC. This avoids having to use a lead or having the adapter protruding well out from the rear of the PC. These days most PCs have a free PCI expansion slot, but USB ports soon seem to be used up.

There are drawbacks as well though, and one of them is that the aerial is not placed in a favourable position. It is in amongst the leads at the rear of the PC. Even if you can manage to keep most of the leads away from

Fig.3.8 A PCI wi-fi card and a tower case is not a good combination

the aerial, it will still be very close to the metal case (Figure 3.8). This situation is considerably less than ideal, and is likely to compromise results. Matters are compounded by the fact that repositioning the aerial to avoid a "blind" spot means moving the entire base unit.

There is a possible solution, but this is dependent on the aerial having a standard fitting and being detachable from the card. Most PCI adaptors do have a standard connector for the aerial, which is easily unscrewed from the card (Figure 3.9). Figure 3.10 shows a close-up of the connectors on the card and the aerial. Note that it is usually necessary to temporarily dismount the aerial so that the card can be installed in the PC.

One way of using the aerial away from the rear of the PC is to use an extension cable. An alternative is to obtain a new aerial complete with cable. The second method is likely to be much more expensive, but it might be possible to obtain an aerial that has a built-in stand so that it is easily mounted on top of a PC, on a desktop, etc. Unfortunately, aerials and extension cables are less widely available than the wi-fi adapters themselves, and they seem to be relatively expensive.

The obvious way of adding a wi-fi adapter is to have a device that connects to a standard Ethernet port. Strangely, I have not encountered a simple adapter that uses this method, although more complex wi-fi devices do use this method of interfacing. There is a drawback to using an Ethernet port for a wi-fi adapter, which is that it is not possible to draw power from

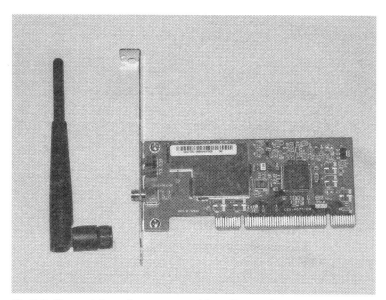

Fig.3.9 The aerial can be unscrewed from the card

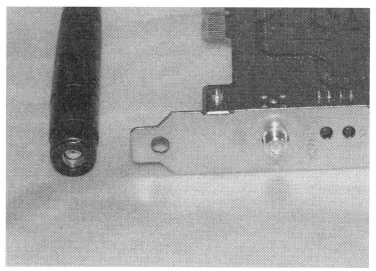

Fig.3.10 Close-up of the connectors on the aerial and the PCI card

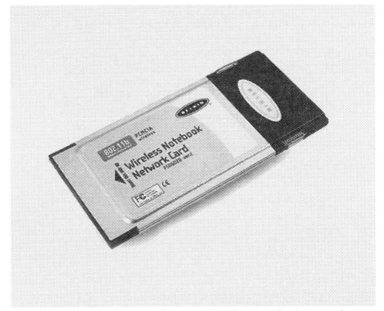

Fig.3.11 A PC card is a popular way of adding a wi-fi adapter to laptop and notebook PCs

this type of port. This would make it necessary to have a mains adapter to power the device, which would be less convenient than drawing power from the PC. Of course, no adapter is needed for PCI or USB wi-fi adapters.

PC card

Some notebook and laptop PCs are now equipped with a wi-fi adaptor as standard, and it is a feature of portable PCs that use Intel's Centrino technology. It is still more usual for any networking capability to be in the form of an ordinary Ethernet port though, although this may change in due course. PCI wi-fi adapters are not useable with portable PCs, but modern laptop and notebook PCs usually have a USB port. This port should work perfectly well with any USB wi-fi adapter. The other option, and probably the more popular one, is to use a "PC" (PCMCIA) card (Figure 3.11). This simply slots into the PCMCIA expansion slot of the portable computer. The aerial is built into the card.

Many small computing devices such as PDAs and Pocket PCs can now have wi-fi connectivity, but you really need to investigate what options (if any) are available for your particular devices. The most common ploy is to have a Compact Flash (CF) card that is actually a wi-fi adapter, such as the Netgear card shown in Figure 3.12. Secure Digital wi-fi cards are also available. Of course, not every gadget that

Fig.3.12 This Netgear CF card is actually a wi-fi adapter

takes one of these memory cards can use the wi-fi versions, so it is important to check compatibility with your portable equipment before buying anything.

Access point

Fitting a PC with a wi-fi adapter gives the wireless equivalent of a PC that has an Ethernet port and a network cable, but with nothing at the other end of the cable. In order to produce a functioning network it is necessary to have a device that will act as a control centre and merge the individual PCs into a proper network. This device is known by a variety of names, but it is mostly called a "base station" or an "access point". The term "access point" is probably the one that is used the most in the UK, and it is the one that will be used in this book.

The exact function of the access point varies somewhat, as it is often merged with other functions such as an ADSL modem to provide an Internet gateway. However, its core function is always to avoid chaos and ensure that each device in the system communicates with the others in an orderly fashion. It receives transmissions from devices in the system and distributes them to the network.

Apparently it is possible to use a PC with a wi-fi adapter as an access point if the PC is equipped with a suitable program. This method seems to be little used in home and small business networks though, and it is not a setup that I have ever used. The more usual approach is to have the access point in the form of a standalone unit, leaving the PCs in the system free to get on with other things.

Ad Hoc

It is not essential to use an access point, and two wi-fi equipped PCs that can receive each others signals can establish a network in what is called "Ad Hoc mode". This is the wi-fi equivalent of two PCs being connected together using their Ethernet ports and a crossed-over cable. The wi-fi version is actually more versatile in that it enables easy communication between any two PCs that are within range, and no cable swapping is required. However, proper networking effectively provides a simultaneous connection between every unit in the system, and is even more versatile. Although it is not without attractions, the Ad Hoc method of networking is inferior to using an access point, and is little used in practice.

Note that when installing and setting up a wi-fi adapter it might be necessary to specify the mode of operation that you wish to use. The adapter's control software then seeks signals from the appropriate type of wi-fi unit. With Ad Hoc mode selected, the software searches for signals from other wi-fi adapters, and will only communicate with that type of unit.

The other mode is called Infrastructure mode, and it is used to implement full networking. Infrastructure mode can only be facilitated with the aid of an access point. Some wi-fi adapters start in what is effectively Ad Hoc mode so that they can search for and list all the available wi-fi signals. By default they will probably connect to and use any access point that is found. As always, it is necessary to read the supplied documentation in order to determine the exact way in which the equipment operates.

As pointed out previously, the main advantage of using Infrastructure mode and an access point is that it enables communications between numerous devices to take place simultaneously. In effect, everything in the network is connected to everything else in the network all the time. In this respect it is the same as a wired network. With Ad Hoc working only two devices can be linked at any one time. Another advantage is that the access point can provide what is termed a "bridge". In other words, it can provide a bridge between wi-fi equipped devices and wired

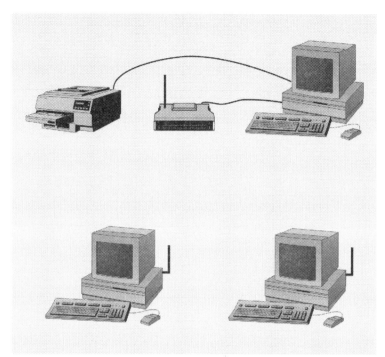

Fig.3.13 A typical wi-fi network has one PC wired to the access point and a printer, with the other PCs networked using wi-fi

network devices. This is an important point, because few practical networks are purely of the wi-fi variety.

Of course, a wi-fi network can be purely that, with everything in the system communicating via radio links. No doubt there are many networks that perform very well using nothing but wi-fi links. In practice though, a totally wi-fi network is unlikely to be the best solution. With the access point on the same desk as one of the PCs, there is little point in using a wi-fi link between the two. A cable will do the job better and at a fraction of the price.

A typical wi-fi network would therefore use a setup of the type shown in Figure 3.13, with one PC wired to the access point and a printer, with the other PCs linked via wi-fi adapters. Apart from file sharing between the PCs in the system, it could also be set up to give all three PCs access to the printer. Obviously this arrangement can be modified to suit individual

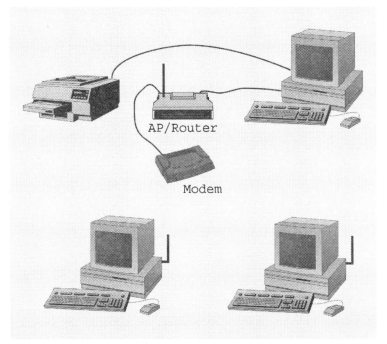

Fig.3.14 A modem connected to the access point and router is the best way of sharing an Internet connection

requirements. For example, there could be other PCs close to the access point, and a wired link might be more practical for these PCs. On the other hand, it could be inconvenient to have the access point very close to any of the PCs in the system, and a fully wi-fi network could then be used.

Internet gateway

The access point can act as a simple hub, but most users opt for a router, which is unlikely to cost much more. If the network will be used to share a broadband Internet connection, it is a good idea to obtain a router that has provision for a modem, or to obtain a router that has a built-in modem. It is not essential to do so, and a setup of the type shown in Figure 3.13 will permit the Internet connection of one PC to be shared.

Fig.3.15 The Netgear WGR614 wi-fi router

However, the modem connects to one of the PCs in the system, and it will only be available if that PC is switched on. The PC connected to the modem becomes a form of router, and handling this task will use a significant proportion of its processing power. A modem connected to a router, or a modem combined in one unit with a router is a much better way of handling things, and any extra cost involved should be minimal.

Things are different with the network of Figure 3.14, where the modem and router would normally be left running 24 hours per day. Any PC in the network can then access the modem via the router regardless of whether any of the other PCs are switched on. Sharing the Internet connection in this fashion does not increase the loading on any PC in the network. The access point and router handle the extra workload of sharing the connection. A combined modem and router usually includes additional facilities such as NAT and a firewall, and it provides what is termed an "Internet gateway". Some of these facilities might be provided by a separate modem and router, but the integrated approach is neater and generally provides the most features.

Using separate units is an attractive proposition if you already have either the modem or the router. This method will only work if the modem and the router are designed to use the same type of interface. This usually means an Ethernet port rather than a USB type. Consequently, if you already have a broadband modem that uses a USB interface it might not be possible to use it in this arrangement. It is certainly worth checking to see what is available, since networking gadgets with new features are appearing all the time. On the other hand, the cost of combined modems and routers has fallen substantially in recent times, and buying one of these units will probably be well worth the small additional outlay.

Wi-fi routers

The Netgear WGR614 wi-fi router (Figure 3.15) is an example of a device that is designed to operate using an external ADSL or cable modem. The rear of this unit is shown in Figure 3.16, and the socket on the extreme left-hand side is for the mains adapter. This unit is fully wi-fi enabled, but the group of four Ethernet sockets permit up to four wired connections to the router. The single Ethernet socket to the right of these handles the connection to the modem.

A typical way of using a router of this type is to disconnect the modem from the PC and connect it to the appropriate Ethernet port of the router instead. A standard Ethernet cable is then used to connect the PC to an Ethernet port in the group of four on the router. This PC can then access the Internet in much the same way as it did previously, as can any other PCs that are wired to the router or use a wi-fi link. The NAT feature of the router ensures that each PC only receives the correct data from the Internet, and to each user it seems as though they have an individual Internet connection. Having the modem connect direct to the router

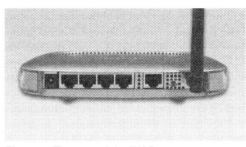

Fig.3.16   The rear of the WGR614

rather than a PC provides a simple form of firewall that hides the PCs from hackers. This type of firewall has its limitations though. A "proper" firewall in the WGR614 helps to keep hackers at bay and will try to thwart DoS (Denial of Service) attacks.

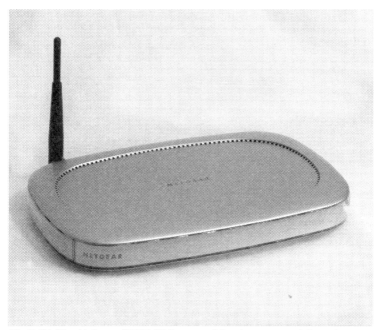

Fig.3.17 The Netgear DG834G is a combined access point, router,
*   ADSL modem, and firewall*

The Netgear DG834G shown in Figure 3.17 is similar to the WGR614 in
that it contains a wi-fi enabled router that also has four ordinary Ethernet
ports for wired connections. Additionally though, it has an integral ADSL
modem. The socket near the right-hand end of the rear panel (Figure
3.18) is not an Ethernet type. It is the type of telephone socket used for
self installed ADSL connections. It is connected to the telephone socket
via the appropriate lead and a microfilter.

Like the DGR614, the DG834G has a NAT feature that makes the routing
"transparent" to users, who each appear to have their own Internet
connection. It also incorporates a fairly sophisticated firewall that gives
protection against DoS (Denial of Service) attacks and uses stateful packet
inspection (SPI) to ensure that received packets of data are in response
to requested data. It is possible to have unrestricted access from the
Internet to one PC, which is necessary for some types of use such as
hosting web services and certain types of peer-to-peer file sharing. It
even incorporates content filtering so that access to certain types of site
can be controlled.

Fig.3.18 The rear of the Netgear DG834G

Installation is largely automatic with the installation program detecting and making the optimum connection to your Internet service provider (ISP). Many complex wi-fi gadgets now largely install themselves, but bear in mind that it is necessary for the user to set up some parameters in order to get the most from the equipment. In particular, the user must set up the wi-fi security measures needed to prevent outsiders using the system for free Internet access, and to keep information on the PCs secure.

Other devices

For many users, all that will be needed are one or two PCs wired to a router and modem, plus a few PCs, PDAs, etc., connected to the network via a wireless link. However, there are plenty of additional wi-fi gadgets available if you should need them. Probably the most popular wi-fi gadgets are the printer adapters. There are actually two wireless options available here, because it is possible to use Bluetooth or wi-fi to provide a cordless connection to a printer.

Bluetooth is the more simple option. One approach would be to have a Bluetooth printer adapter fitted to the printer, or to use a printer that has this facility built-in (assuming you can find one). Each PC could then have a Bluetooth adapter to give it access to the printer. With the PCs already networked, this definitely seems to be doing things the hard way.

It would have the advantage of making the printer available at any time, and access to it would not be dependent on a certain PC being operational at the time. The main drawback is that it would be adding a wireless network to a system that already had a wireless network, which would be a complicated and expensive way of doing things. In theory, the Bluetooth equipment should manage to channel hop and avoid any major interference between the two systems, but in practice there would be a slight risk of the wi-fi network's performance suffering.

With an existing wi-fi network in place, there are several ways of sharing a printer. As standard, Windows permits any printer connected to any PC to be shared with all the other PCs in the network, and no additional software is required. With the printer connected to one of the PCs, it can be set as a shared resource and used by any PC in the system provided the host PC is switched on. The obvious drawback of this system is that it might be necessary to keep switching on a PC simply to permit users of other PCs to access a printer. The big advantage is that it requires no additional hardware, and it enables a printer to be networked at zero cost.

Printer servers

Another option is to have the printer connected to the network via a wired or wi-fi network printer server. This is effectively an extremely basic computer that enables a printer to connect direct to the network via an Ethernet port or a wi-fi link. In fact some of these units have support for two or more printers. The advantage of these devices is that they can be left running continuously at practically no cost, making the supported printer or printers always available.

The principal drawback is that printer servers are not particularly cheap. When used with a low-cost inkjet printer it is likely that the printer server would cost more than the printer. Some of these devices do not support all the features of the printer due to a lack of bidirectional operation. In other words, the PCs can send data to the printer, but the printer might not be able to send back information such as the amount of ink left in the cartridges. In most cases the printer is still perfectly usable though. Printer servers often have only one type of printer interface, so make sure that it is the right type if your printer also has only a single interface.

Fig.3.19 The HP 5850 printer has a built-in 802.11b wi-fi adapter

Many up-market printers have a built-in printer server or it is available as an optional extra. Practically every printer intended for the corporate market has this feature, and few big business users would seriously consider a printer that was not capable of network operation. Few printers for home and small business use have network connectivity as standard, and it is not really a common option either. It is a feature of a few printers though, and the HP 5850 inkjet printer (Figure 3.19) has a built-in 802.11b wi-fi adapter. As one would reasonably expect, Ethernet and wi-fi connectivity significantly add to the cost of a printer, but also add greatly to its flexibility.

Note that it is not just printers that can be connected direct to the network. It is also possible to share scanners and multifunction devices, and possibly other gadgets as well. The choice is relatively limited though, and it tends to be only the more upmarket "professional" equipment that offers network connectivity. Although the Windows XP Help system seems to suggest that there is built-in support for sharing scanners, this is not actually the case. There is only built-in support for sharing printers, and you need additional software in order to use ordinary scanners via a network.

Extending range

As explained previously, the theoretical range of a wi-fi system and the real-world range are often very different, with the range obtained in practice tending to fall short of the theoretical maximum. In some cases it falls well short of the theoretical maximum. This does not necessarily matter, and in many situations there is no need for a large operating range. Unless a wi-fi system is being installed in a very large building, trying to stretch the system to its limits is unnecessary. However, there are gadgets available if you should need to extend the range of a link in the system.

Some of this equipment is fairly straightforward, such as aerials for outdoor use. Operating from one building to another often produces poor results even though the aerials seem to be within range. This problem is due to the use of indoor aerials that require the signal to go through at least two walls on its way from one end of the link to the other. The signal absorption can be quite high, giving a much lower than expected range.

By having both aerials outside it is often possible to have "clear air" between them, and something in the region of the full 100 metre operating range should be obtained. A significantly longer range is possible if reduced operating speed can be tolerated, but it is probably best not to take some of the claims for these aerials too seriously. For one thing, the greater the operating range, the lower the chance of having a path between the aerials that is totally clear of obstructions.

Directional

The simple aerials normally used with wi-fi networks are omnidirectional, which means that they transmit with equal strength in all directions. When receiving signals, they are equally sensitive in all directions. The omnidirectional term is not strictly accurate, because immediately above and below the aerial (which should be vertical) there are two "blind" spots. With most types of radio communication this is unimportant, but it should be borne in mind when installing a wi-fi network on two or more floors of a building.

In addition to the "blind" spots, signal strengths tend to be reduced when an aerial is higher or lower than the aerial at the access point. The range obtained on floors above and below the access point could therefore be less than the range obtained on the same floor. In fact this is almost certain to occur, because there is the added signal absorption of the floors and ceilings when a link is established between different levels of a building. These factors almost certainly account for the disappointing results that are sometimes obtained when using wi-fi equipment in a multi-storey building.

A directional aerial gives better results in one or possibly two directions. With several pieces of equipment using a wi-fi link to the network, omnidirectional operation is essential for the access point. It has to communicate with various pieces of equipment scattered around the building. It is highly unlikely that they will be conveniently placed so that they are all in more or less the same direction relative to the access point.

The situation is different when there are only two devices to be linked. A directional aerial is then acceptable at both ends of the link. When there are more than two wi-fi units in a network, a directional aerial can normally be used for anything other than the access point. Unless Ad Hoc operation is used, all the other devices in the system communicate via the access point, and do not directly communicate with anything else in the network. They can therefore communicate with the network by way a directional aerial aimed at the access point.

We are all familiar with directional aerials. Ordinary television aerials and satellite dishes are common examples of directional aerials, and for good results they have to be aimed quite accurately at the transmitter or satellite. The point of a directional aerial is that it provides gain. In other words, using a directional aerial produces a stronger signal when transmitting. A stronger transmission in one direction is obtained by having a weaker signal radiated in other directions. Increased sensitivity is obtained when a directional aerial is used for reception, but only in one direction. The sensitivity of the aerial is lower in all other directions. The more highly directional an aerial is made, the greater the gain that can be obtained.

Using a directional aerial can significantly increase the operating range of a wi-fi system, but it also makes it more difficult to get everything set up correctly and working well. Also, directional aerials are relatively difficult to obtain and expensive. It might be necessary to search online for a specialist supplier of wi-fi equipment in order to find something that suits your requirements.

Try to organise the network in a way that minimises the risk of range problems occurring. The access point should be somewhere near the middle of the building so that it is reasonably close to all the wi-fi enabled

Fig.3.20 This unit provides a wi-fi link from a PC to a hi-fi system

devices. Having the access point at one end of the building maximises the chances of problems, especially where there will be one of more wi-fi devices at the other end of the building.

The rest

An access point, some wi-fi adapters, and possibly a printer sharer or two, are all that is necessary for normal networking. Not surprisingly perhaps, the designers of computing equipment have come up with various other wi-fi gadgets to make your network even more useful. Some of these units will probably sink without trace in due course, but a few provide genuinely useful functions.

With PCs being used increasingly for entertainment purposes, and in particular for playing and managing audio files, a wi-fi link between your computer network and hi-fi system is potentially very useful. In fact there does not have to be a network, and a wi-fi link between a standalone PC and a hi-fi system could be very useful. Units of this type sometimes have a built-in display, like the one on the Slim Devices Squeezebox (Figure 3.20). The alternative is to use a television set to provide the display so that audio files on the network can be listed, and the desired files then selected. There is usually the option of playing the files via the sound system of the television.

It should be possible to use essentially the same method to link Mpeg and other types of video file to a television set. I am not aware of a unit that will do this, but it is possible to obtain a webcam that has a built-in server and 802.11g wi-fi adapter. The Linksys Wireless-g Internet Video Camera is an example of a wi-fi webcam. A large bandwidth is needed for even the low resolution output of a webcam, and the Linksys unit therefore uses a 802.11g wi-fi link. It can handle a respectable maximum resolution of 640 by 480 pixels and it has a sound channel.

On the face of it, this is an application that is ideal for a Bluetooth link, with its low power consumption. The relatively low bandwidth would limit the performance, but most webcams use a USB 1.1 interface, which has a similar bandwidth. Surprisingly perhaps, I can not find any Bluetooth Webcams for sale.

Accelerators

The maximum speed possible using 802.11 wi-fi equipment is the 54Mbits per second provided by 802.11g equipment, but you might find equipment advertised as offering something more like 100 or 108Mbits per second. The increase in speed is obtained by using some form of accelerator technology, which seems to mean changes to the way in which the packets of data are encoded and decoded. The radio side of things is just uses standard 802.11 technology. Faster versions of 802.11b and 802.11g devices are produced. Note that in order to take advantage of the speed increase it is necessary for all the wi-fi devices in the network to use the same accelerator technology.

Points to remember

A basic wireless adapter for a desktop PC can be in the form of a PCI expansion card or an external USB device. USB 2.0 is required in order to make full use of the speed available from an 802.11g adapter. The obvious method of interfacing via an Ethernet port seems to be little used in practice. Most USB wi-fi adapters will not work in conjunction with a passive USB hub.

A notebook or laptop PC can be interfaced to a basic wi-fi adapter using a USB port, but a PC card is the more popular choice. Some other portable computing devices can be wi-fi enabled, and a common ploy is to use a special version of a Compact Flash card. Many of these wi-fi gadgets only suit a limited range of devices, so always check compatibility with your particular PDA (or whatever) before buying anything.

Most practical wi-fi networks are based on a device called an access point. This acts as a sort of control centre, with all other devices in the network communicating via the access point rather than directly. The access point often provides other facilities, such as bridging to wired network devices, a firewall, and possibly even an ADSL broadband modem.

Any printer connected to a PC in the system can be set as a shared resource so that it can be used with other PCs in the network. This avoids the need for any additional hardware, but the printer will only be available if the PC driving it is switched on. A printer server enables a printer to be connected direct to the network so that it is always available.

Bluetooth can provide a cordless connection from a PC to a printer, or from several PCs to a single printer. Providing access to a printer via the main network is a simpler and cheaper way of handling things though.

It is possible to network devices without using an access point, and this method relies on using the Ad Hoc mode of operation. This gives only a very simple form of networking, with two devices at a time communicating directly. Consequently, this mode is little used in practice.

A directional aerial can be used to extend the range of a wi-fi network, but the aerial for the access point normally has to be an omnidirectional type. Having the access point near the middle of the network helps to avoid problems with inadequate range.

There are numerous wi-fi units that provide functions which you never knew you needed! Some of the more specialised units are genuinely useful, such as wi-fi units that enable audio files stored on a computer to be played on a hi-fi system.

4

Installation
and security

Installation

Before installing any computer hardware, including Ethernet and wi-fi
devices, it is essential to read the instruction manual. Realising that few
people can be bothered to read the manual, many manufacturers now
include a "Quick Start" leaflet, or something similar. At the very least you
should look through the leaflet to determine the recommended method
of installation. Failure to do so can result in a lot of wasted time due to a
failed initial installation, and everything then having to be uninstalled and
reinstalled correctly. With the more awkward devices it can be difficult
and time consuming to get everything working once an installation has
failed. Windows just keeps going back to the incorrect version despite
your best efforts.

It is increasingly common for manufacturers to recommend that the
software is installed first, with the hardware being added once the drivers
are safely installed. In theory it should be perfectly all right for the
hardware to be fitted first. The Plug and Play facility of Windows should
then find the hardware and install the driver software. In practice this
method can be problematic, with Windows trying to install the wrong
drivers, failing to recognise the right drivers, or continually detecting the
hardware and trying to install the already installed drivers. Following the
manufacturer's installation instructions "to the letter" should minimise
the risk of running into problems with the drivers.

It would seem reasonable to assume that the drivers supplied with the
new hardware will be fully tested and working. Matters are often very
different in practice, with minor problems often occurring when the
supplied drivers are used with some PCs. Also, it has been known for
manufacturers to rush out new hardware with the drivers not being tested
as comprehensively as they should be. This can cause major problems
for anyone that tries to install them. I have obtained one or two pieces of

cheap generic hardware where the supplied discs were clearly for another, and totally different piece of hardware!

It is a good idea to search the manufacturer's web site for any updated drivers before trying to install any new hardware. If you do find more recent drivers, read any installation instructions that come with them. The installation method often differs from that for the drivers supplied with the hardware. Even where the supplied drivers work all right, there might be improved drivers that provide more features, faster operation, or whatever. It is always a good idea to use the latest driver software that can be found.

In the case of generic hardware there might not be a manufacturer's web site where you can seek new drivers and other support. The drivers supplied with this type of software are often those provided by the producer of the chips on which the hardware is based. A computer chip manufacturer's web site will usually have the latest drivers for their products. Failing that, the retailer's customer support service is the only hope. Generic hardware is cheap, but you are unlikely to obtain the same sort of support that is available when "big name" products are purchased.

Firmware

With the more complex networking equipment you will sometimes find that there is more than just improved driver software available. Complex networking devices such as combined routers and modems are based on a microcontroller, which is essentially a fairly basic but capable computer on a single chip. This computer runs a program that is built into the hardware. Because the program is a mixture of hardware and software it is usually termed "firmware".

In addition to improved driver software it is now quite common for manufacturers to make better firmware available. The firmware is usually stored in some form of flash memory. Unlike normal computer memory, this type retains its contents when the equipment is switched off, but it can still be reprogrammed. Sometimes the firmware upgrades provide improved performance or extra features, but they are mostly used to fix minor bugs.

It is certainly a good idea to look for firmware upgrades and install any that you find. A firmware upgrade is not something to be undertaken lightly though, and mistakes can render the equipment unusable. Read the manufacturers installation instructions very carefully at least once, and follow them precisely. Installing new firmware is usually a very simple process and it should all go smoothly provided silly mistakes are avoided. Probably the most popular silly mistake is to download the wrong upgrade. Computing equipment tends to be sold under a range of similar names and numbers, so be careful to ensure that the download is for the exact piece of equipment you are using.

A manufacturer sometimes recommends installing a firmware upgrade before using a piece of equipment in earnest. This is unusual though, and usually means that a serious bug has been found in the original firmware. Unless an equipment manufacturer recommends otherwise, it is probably best to get the equipment installed and working before undertaking any firmware upgrades. A detailed description of downloading and installing new firmware is covered at the end of this chapter.

Setting up

Both wired and wi-fi networking equipment can require a lot of complex setting up before it is ready for use. Fortunately, the equipment manufacturers have realised that most users would prefer not to spend months becoming an expert on networks just so that they can install and set up a simple home or small business network. Consequently, practically all modern networking equipment is supplied with drivers and other software that makes setting up and using the network as simple as possible. The installation software will usually scan the PC, Internet connection, etc., and then go through a largely automatic setting up procedure. There could still be some work to do in order to get things working really well and securely.

It is advisable to install the access point before adding anything else to the network. In general, wi-fi adapters are very easy to install, and the process is largely automatic. However, without an access point to communicate with it is difficult for a wi-fi adapter to set itself up correctly and do anything worthwhile. It is assumed here, that there will be at least one PC that has a wired connection to the access point. In a fully wi-fi network it is clearly necessary to have at least one PC with an installed wi-fi adapter before it is possible to contact and set up the access point. It is still probably best to have the access point switched on before installing the wi-fi adapters, but it is advisable to check the access point's instruction manual for guidance on this matter.

Setting up the access point is different depending on whether it is an add-on to an existing wired network, a type having a built-in router, or

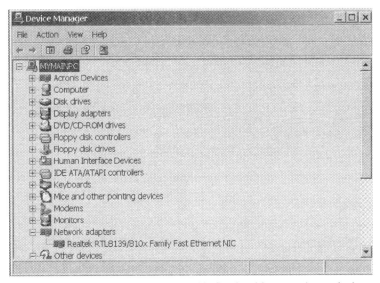

*Fig.4.1 The Ethernet adapter is listed in Device Manager, but a device
such as a router or access point will not be found here*

one having both a router and broadband modem. The process also
varies somewhat from one manufacturer to another, and can even be
different for various models from the same manufacturer. One example
is provided here, and it demonstrates some basic principles, but it is
essential to read the instruction manuals before installing any wi-fi
equipment. The manuals should give concise guidance and fully explain
any unusual aspects of installation. The examples given here can do no
more than give some idea of the stages involved in setting up a wi-fi
network.

Standalone

It is important to realise that the access point is unlikely to appear in the
list of installed units in Device Manager. As part of the setting up process
you might have to install a control program for the access point on one
of the PCs, but this will be an ordinary piece of software and not a set of
device drivers. After installing new hardware it is normal to look for its
entry in Device Manager to check that there are no problems. Looking
in the Network Adapters section of Device Manager will show an entry

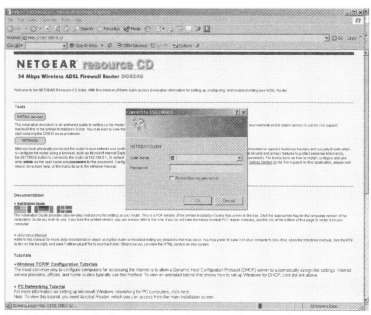

Fig.4.2 The supplied username and password are required in order to start the web-based configuration process

for the Ethernet or wi-fi adapter fitted to that PC (Figure 4.1), but there will be no entry for the access point.

The reason for this is simply that the access point is not a device installed on one of the PCs. It has its own built-in microcontroller, and it has to be regarded as akin to a PC in the system. The same is true of a printer server and any other standalone units in the system. Obviously it is necessary to have some means of making adjustments to the access point's settings, and this is normally achieved either using a control program in one of the networked PCs or using web-based configuration software. Either way the process is usually handled by a wizard, and will probably be largely automatic. It is probably best to avoid units that do not offer a user-friendly method of installation and setting up.

The so-called web-based method of configuration is increasingly common, and as such it does not use a configuration program in one of the networked PCs. Instead, you run a browser program such as Internet Explorer, and then use a special web address. It then appears as though you are configuring the device via a series of web pages, but these pages

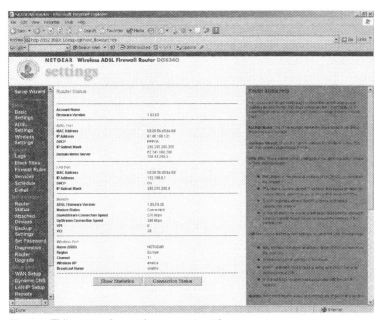

Fig.4.3 This page shows the current settings

are embedded within the device's firmware, as is any supporting software for them. The configuration is therefore achieved using an ordinary browser running on one of the networked PCs, together with firmware within the access point.

Settings

A web-based setup program is used for the Netgear DG834G, which is an all-in-one 802.11g access point, ADSL modem, router, and firewall. The setup pages can be accessed by typing the appropriate address into a browser, or by clicking the link on the page that is launched when the installation disc is run. Either way, it is necessary to use the supplied username and password when prompted (Figure 4.2). The initial setting up procedure is largely automatic, but with a device that contains a modem it is necessary to supply basic connection information, such as the username and password for your broadband account. This information should have been provided by your Internet service provider (ISP) when you signed on to the account.

The connection information is stored in the modem and there is no need for you to provide it in order to gain access to the Internet. Normally the unit is left running continuously, so once it has connected to the Internet it stays connected. Any PC in the network then has instant access to the Internet at any time. Of course, things can go wrong, and over a period of time it is likely that for one reason or another, the

Fig.4.4 The Connection Status window

Internet connection will be lost. Switching the unit off, waiting a few seconds, and then switching it on again will force it to reconnect, using the stored username, password, and other connection data.

A page like the one in Figure 4.3 is displayed once the initial setting up has been completed. This page shows the current settings in the main section, and there are some menus in the right-hand section. A scrollable Help page is available on the opposite side of the screen. Operating the Connection Status button near the bottom of the screen produces the

small window shown in Figure 4.4. This confirms that a connection to the Internet has been made, and provides two buttons that enable the modem to be disconnected and reconnected. The Show Statistics button produce a small window like the

Fig.4.5 The Router Statistics window

101

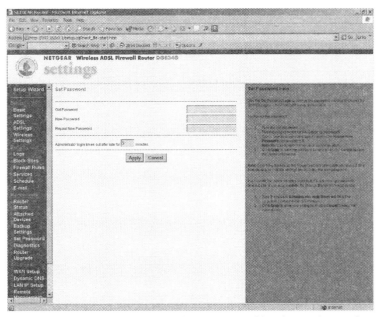

Fig.4.6 The unit is not secure until the password has been changed

one of Figure 4.5, which shows things like the number of data packets handled by various parts of the system.

It is the menus down the left of the screen that are of importance in the current context, as these give access to screens that control numerous settings. Most of these should not be altered, and it is definitely not a good idea to start experimenting with settings that you do not understand. There are some settings that can be usefully altered though, and one of these is the password used to access the setup pages. The default password is the same for every unit, so you must change it in order to genuinely password protect the system. Operating the Password menu option brings up the page of Figure 4.6. This operates in the standard fashion, with the old and new passwords being entered, followed by the new password again in case a mistake was made the first time.

Security

Note that this password is the one used to gain access to the setup program so that changes can be made to the configuration of the modem,

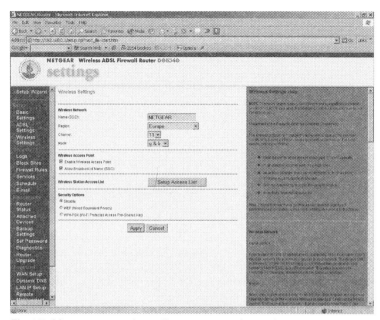

Fig.4.7 Most access points offer two types of security

router, etc. This password does not provide protection against hackers gaining access to the network via a wi-fi link. Any reasonably modern access point should offer at least two types of protection against hackers, and in this case the security settings are accessed via Wireless Options in the Setup menu. This brings up the page shown in Figure 4.7.

Most of the settings here are the basic ones for a wi-fi link, such as the region, channel number, and name of the access point. It is not essential to change the name, but there is obviously scope for confusion if you live in an area that has several wi-fi networks in operation. With everyone using the default name it is likely that the same name will be used for two access points in the same area.

The DG834G is an 802.11g device, and as such it is compatible with 802.11b units. One of the menus enables it to be restricted to 802.11b or 802.11g operation. It can be advantageous to change the channel used by the system, and the reasons for this are discussed in the next chapter. The rest of the system adjusts to the channel used by the access point, so changing the channel used by the access point effectively changes the channel used by the entire network.

Three security options are available in the lower part of the screen, and the default option is for security measures to be disabled. It is best to use this setting initially, since it gives unrestricted access to the system, making it easy to get it working with the other wi-fi units in the network. It is important to implement one of the security measures at an early stage though, especially if the PCs in the network are used for anything where security is important. This includes online ordering of goods and services, online auctions, Internet banking or other online financial dealing, and private correspondence.

WEP

The original and most basic form of wi-fi security is called Wired Equivalent Privacy, or WEP. This has been used with wi-fi equipment from the outset, and it is based on an encryption and decryption technique. The idea was to make wi-fi links as secure as the wired variety, and it is from this that the name of the system is derived. For WEP to work it is necessary for each wi-fi unit to have it enabled and to use the same key. The key is a large number used in the encryption and decryption process, and it is the WEP equivalent of a password.

An advantage of WEP is that any wi-fi gadget should be capable of using this security system, regardless of its precise function and which company produced it. Note that WEP is only used for wi-fi links and not for the wired variety, which are intrinsically more secure. Even where a network has a mixture of wired and wireless links, WEP security will only be used for the wireless links. Also note that the encryption and decryption process will reduce the speed of data transfers.

The level of security obtained depends on the number of bits used by the encryption process. Older equipment sometimes supports nothing beyond 64-bit operation, but modern wi-fi devices support at least 128-bit encryption. Obviously you should use the highest level of encryption that your equipment supports, but note that all the devices must use the same level. If some devices support 256-bit operation while others offer no more than 128-bit encryption, the whole system has to use 128-bit encryption.

In the DG834G setup program, the bottom section of the page changes when the WEP option is selected, with some new menus and textboxes appearing (Figure 4.8). One of the menus offers 64-bit or 128-bit encoding, and provided the other wi-fi units support it, 128-bit encoding should be used. The encoding type can be either Open System or Shared

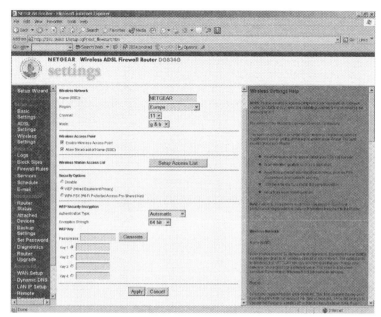

Fig.4.8 Selecting WEP security produces further options

Key, and all units in the system must use the same setting. In this case there is an automatic option as the default. This can be changed to one of the other settings if automatic operation fails to work properly.

A WEP key can be generated by typing a short phrase into the appropriate textbox and operating the Generate key. Four keys are produced for 64-bit operation, but only one is generated for 128-bit encryption. The key will usually be in hexadecimal, which means that it will be comprised of numbers from 0 to 9 plus the first six letters of the alphabet (A to F). If it is generated in the form of a hexadecimal number by the access point's software, make sure that the software for your wi-fi adapters is set up to accept the key in the same form.

WPA

While WEP is adequate to keep casual hackers out of a home or small business network, it is vulnerable to determined hackers armed with the appropriate tools. This deterred larger business users from installing wi-

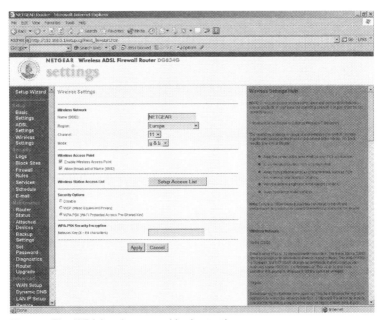

Fig.4.9 The WPA key is entered in the textbox

fi links in their networks. With systems carrying sensitive information that could be worth millions to competitors, it was clearly not a good idea to use links that were anything less than totally secure. The equipment manufacturers' answer to this problem was a new and improved form of security called WPA-PSK (Wi-Fi Protected Access Pre-Shared Key). These days it is often just called WPA.

In this example there is a WPA-PSK security option, and selecting it produces a textbox (Figure 4.9) where the net key is added. This must be at least 8 characters, and can be up to 32 ASCII characters (numbers, letters, etc.) or up to 64 hexadecimal digits (0 to 9 and A to F). One reason for the better security provided by WPA is that the user enters the same key when setting up the network, but the key used for encryption and decryption is periodically changed by the system. The idea is that it is more difficult to find patterns that give away the key if it is changed from time to time. Also, by the time a hacker has found a key it is likely that the system will no longer be using it.

It is clearly a good idea to use WPA where it is felt that the basic security provided by WEP is inadequate, but there can be practical difficulties in

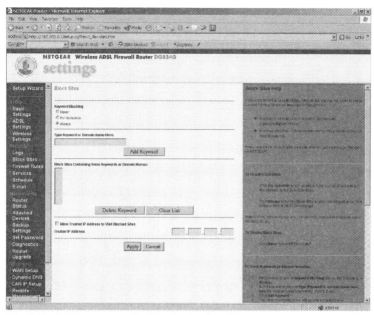

Fig.4.10 Addresses can be blocked using this page

using WPA. The obvious one is that it is not part of the original wi-fi scheme of things, and it is not available with all wi-fi units. Note though, that it might be possible to add this facility via a firmware download.

802.11i

WPA was produced by the Wi-Fi Alliance rather than by the IEEE, and as such it does not form part of any 802.11 standard. The IEEE has been working on the problem of security, and during the course of writing this book its solution was finalised. It is known as 802.11i, but this is not a wi-fi standard of the same type as the other 802.11 standards. It is concerned with security and not with frequencies, transfer speeds, and the like.

Commenting on 802.11i is difficult because there are no products that use it available in the shops at the time of writing this piece. No doubt 802.11i devices will be available by the time you read this, and it will probably be available as a firmware upgrade for some existing products. It should be an improvement compared to both WEP and WPA, and is

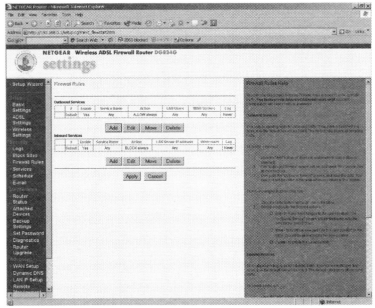

Fig.4.11 This page is used to edit or add firewall rules

the obvious security system to use provided your equipment supports it. Where optimum security is of paramount importance it clearly makes sense to obtain equipment that does support the 802.11i standard.

Other settings

There will probably be other types of setting available via the configuration program, and there could be large numbers of them if the access point includes features such as a built-in modem and firewall. Most of these can simply be left at the default settings, and you should definitely not "play" with them. It is worth investigating any firewall settings, and it might be necessary to adjust these in order to get everything working in a fashion that suits the way you use the Internet. Even if the default settings prove satisfactory, there could be some useful additional features available from the firewall.

The DG834G has the ability to provide some basic content filtering. It can be set to block sites that contain a certain text string in the domain

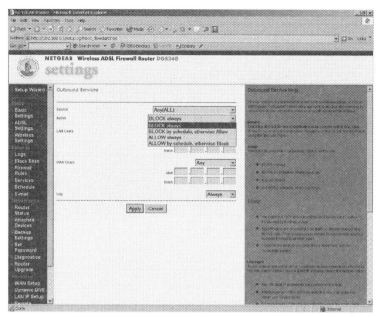

Fig.4.12 This page is used when defining your own firewall rules

name, or it can block specified addresses (Figure 4.10). A specified PC in the network can be given access to the blocked sites. Further control over the firewall is provided by the Firewall Rules page (Figure 4.11). The existing rules can be edited and it is also possible to add your own (Figure 4.12). It sometimes necessary to add rules or alter the existing rules in order to make firewalls work successfully with services such as video conferencing, and some peer-to-peer file sharing systems.

Adapter installation

Installing a wi-fi adapter is usually more straightforward than installing an access point, because the adapter is much more limited in scope. An access point is "its own boss", and often acts as much more than just an access point. A wi-fi adapter is just an ordinary peripheral, and it is essentially just a wireless version of an Ethernet port. Unlike an access point, a wi-fi adapter is installed in the normal fashion, it will use device drivers, and it will have an entry in Device Manager.

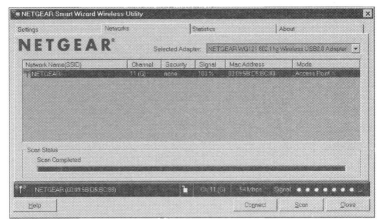

Fig.4.13 The program scans for access points

Before installing any PC add-on it is advisable to check the manufacturer's web site for updated drivers. Most device drivers seem to go through various changes during the lifetime of the supported products. Follow the installation instructions "to the letter", especially when dealing with USB devices, which can be a little pernickety.

Note that it is not necessary to remove an Ethernet card or switch off a built-in Ethernet port in order to install a wi-fi adapter. The two can successfully coexist in the same computer, but obviously you should only use one or the other to connect to the network. There is a slight advantage in removing or switching off the Ethernet port. Leaving an Ethernet adapter installed and operational results in the computer's resources being consumed by a port that is not used. On the other hand, having a working Ethernet port in each PC and a long network cable is useful insurance. If a wi-fi link becomes troublesome, a wired connection can be used until the problem has been sorted out.

Control program

Double-clicking on the adapter's entry in Device Manager will bring up a properties window, and this might have sections that give control over such things as the default channel, the country setting, and the network type. Clearly this is very useful, but it is not used for everyday control of the adapter. There will be a control program that scans the band for

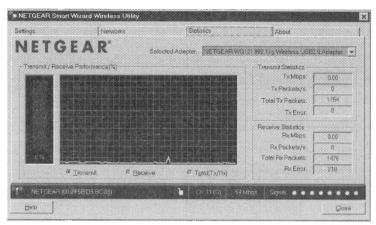

Fig.4.14 The Statistics section includes a graph showing the amount
of data that has passed through the link

access points and will automatically connect to the network if it finds the
correct access point. This might be the only means of controlling the
adapter. The control programs are all different, but some basic features
are common to all of them.

Figure 4.13 shows the control program for the Netgear WG121 802.11g
wi-fi adapter. This program has four sections, and the four tabs near the
top of the window are used to switch between them. The Networks

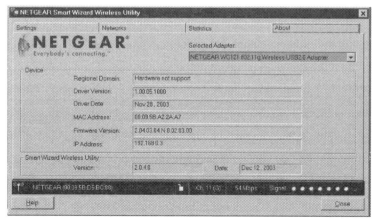

Fig.4.15 This section gives information such as the firmware version

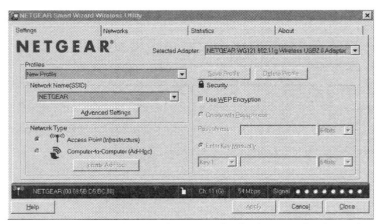

Fig.4.16 As one would probably expect, the Settings section is used to control the operating mode and other important settings

section is shown in Figure 4.13, and this scans for networks and lists those that are found. In this case just one network has been located. The information on this page shows that it is operating on channel 11, it is being received at full strength, and that the connection is operating at the full 54Mbits per second. It also shows that this network is not using any form of security (encryption). Two of the buttons at the bottom of the screen enable the band to be scanned again, and the PC to be connected to the selected network.

The statistics page (Figure 4.14) provides information such as the number of packets that have been received. There is also a display that provides a graph showing the amount of activity, and a bargraph that shows the percentage of the adapter's capacity that is being used. The About section (Figure 4.15) just gives some basic information about the adapter, such as its firmware version and driver details. This information will be needed if you look for updated drivers or firmware on the manufacturer's web site. Note that details of the current drivers can be obtained from the relevant section in Device Manager, but the firmware version is unlikely to be included here.

The Settings section (Figure 4.16) is an important one that controls a number of vital parameters. You can select Infrastructure mode for operation with an access point, or Ad Hoc mode for direct connection to another PC. The ability to define profiles is a standard feature, and one that is supported by this software. The idea is to have a profile defined

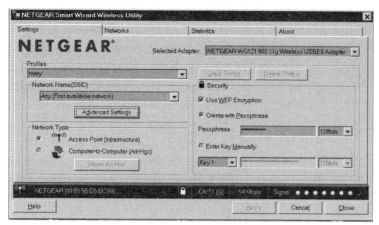

Fig.4.17 This control program includes a "passphrase" facility

for each network that you use. You can then switch from one network to another by selecting the appropriate profile.

Obviously a desktop PC will normally be used with a single network. It could still be useful to define a profile for that network. If there should be other networks within range, the program will automatically connect to the one for which there is a profile, and it will ignore the others. If encryption is introduced at an access point it will be necessary to set the same encryption in the profile for that access point. In this example it was WEP encryption that was activated at the access point. WEP encryption with the same network key must therefore be activated on this adapter, and the others in the system.

WEP is actually the only security option offered by this adapter, and the others in the system. This renders the WPA option at the access point of no practical value. In order to activate WEP encryption at this adapter it is necessary to first tick the Use WEP Encryption checkbox. Then 64-bit or 128-bit operation is selected using the small pop-down menu. Like the access point, this adapter is made by Netgear, and it offers the same "passphrase" method of entering the net key. It is just a matter of operating the upper radio button and entering the same text string that was used at the access point. The software then converts this into the appropriate key and enters it in the text box (Figure 4.17). Manual entry of the key is also possible. Operate the lower radio button and type the network key into the textbox.

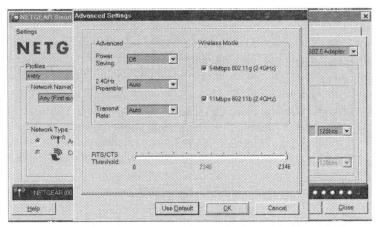

Fig.4.18 802.11b and 802.11g modes are both enabled by default

Operating the Advanced button brings up another window that offers further settings (Figure 4.18). There is probably little here that can be usefully altered though. The two checkboxes enable 802.11b and 802.11g operation to be enabled or disabled.

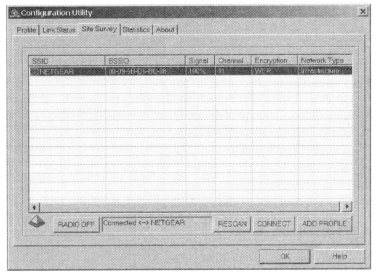

Fig.4.19 This control program also scans for access points

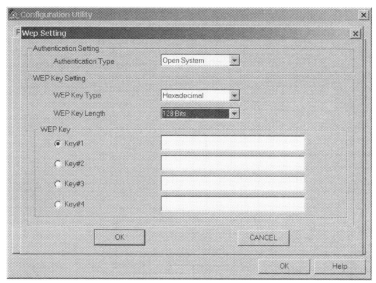

Fig.4.20 This window is used to enter the WEP key

Another PC in the example network has a generic PCI adapter, and this also has software that can scan for access points (Figure 4.19). In order to make a connection to a network it is just a matter of selecting its entry in the main part of the window and then operating the Connect button. It will be necessary to enter the network key if the access point uses WEP security (Figure 4.20). In this case there is no "passphrase" option, and it is a matter of selecting 64-bit or 128-bit operation and then typing the key into the textbox.

The software has support for profiles, and a new profile can be added by selecting a network and then operating the Add Profile button. If WEP security is used, it is necessary to add the network key into the window that pops up. However, the key is stored as part of the profile, and the network can be accessed thereafter without having to enter the key again. The newly added profile should be listed on the appropriate page of the program (Figure 4.21).

Sharing

With the access point set up correctly, the wired and wi-fi links in place, and everything working nicely, the network is in a sense fully operational.

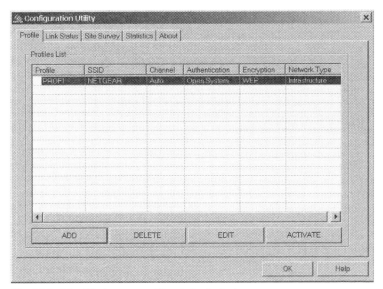

Fig.4.21 A facility to use profiles is included

As things stand it has only one minor drawback, which is that it is not possible to share any resources such as files and printers. The resource sharing facilities built into any modern version of Windows are sufficient for most users, so there should be no need to buy any networking software. However, it is essential to get Windows set up correctly in order to get the network to do anything useful.

When Windows is configured and set up correctly, the shared resources can be used on any PC in the system in the same way as if they were actually part of that PC and its peripherals. Shared files and folders on other computers, for example, can be accessed using Windows Explorer, or via the standard file browsers built into applications software. They appear in the My Network Places folder, but not all the files and folders on other PCs in the network will appear here. Resources are only shared if they are specifically designated as shared resources.

Although most programs will use shared files and folders just as if they were on a local drive, there are actually a few applications programs that will not use them, or will do so in a restricted fashion. Sometimes restrictions on the use of shared files are due to security issues. In other cases it is simply that the speed of the network is inadequate. For example, burning a CD-ROM using data obtained via a wi-fi link might provide an inadequate flow of data, even at fairly low burn speeds. In order to burn a CD-ROM using data obtained over the network it would probably be necessary to copy the data to a local drive first. It would then be transferred to a CD-ROM from the local drive, after which the file on the local drive could be deleted.

Disc sharing

Although it would in many ways be easier if all the hard discs in the system were shared in their entirety, this is definitely not considered to be a good idea. It is actually much easier to use the network if files that will be shared are kept in a few special folders. This makes it easy and quick to find the files that you require. With access to all the folders on every hard disc in the network it could take a long time to locate the particular files you require. The sheer number of files and folders would make finding the right files a bit like "looking for a needle in a haystack". Another important point is that users of the system will probably not wish to make all their files available to the network. Most of us would prefer to keep most files private and only share certain material.

It is particularly important not to share all the files and folders if the network has an Internet connection, which in practice means practically every network. The problem with sharing everything in the system, or even large parts of the system, is that it makes life very easy for anyone who manages to hack into the network. With large-scale or even total access to the system, they will probably be able to steal any files that take their fancy, and damage any files at will. For security reasons it is best to share the minimum amount of files and folders that permits the network to be used efficiently.

Naming

Each computer in the network has to be given a computer name, and each group of computers has a workgroup name. The computers will appear in file browsers under their computer names, and will look much the same as folders. On opening the "folder" for a computer on the network you will only see files and folders that have been designated as shared resources. All other files and folders on the computer are invisible to the network, and they can not be accessed by other computers in the network. Workgroup names are only of significance when networks are networked, but each workgroup must always be named.

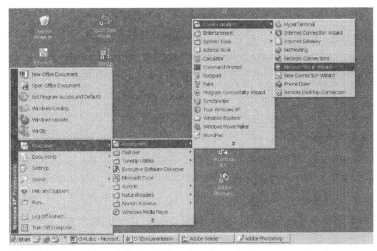

Fig.4.22 The Network Setup Wizard is deep in the menu structure

When selecting names it is essential to choose a different name for each PC. Apart from the fact that having two computers operating under the same name would be confusing for users of the system, it more or less guarantees that the network will not operate reliably. Having two PCs operating under the same name would be equally confusing for Windows! The names can have up to 15 characters, which should be letters and numbers. Spaces are not permitted, but the underline character can be used. Therefore, naming a PC "My Old PC" would not be allowed, but it could be called "My_Old_PC". Although up to 15 characters can be used, it is more practical to settle for a maximum of eight or so. Use names that will enable every user of the network to easily associate each name with the PC it represents.

Network Setup Wizard

The easy way to set up networking on PCs running Windows XP and ME is to run the Network Setup Wizard. This is buried quite deep in the menu structure, but it can be accessed by going to the Start menu and then selecting Programs, Accessories, Communications, and Network Setup Wizard (Figure 4.22). The Windows XP and ME versions are slightly different in points of detail, but they are very similar. The Windows XP version is used as the basis off this example.

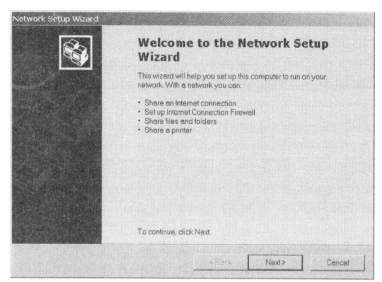

Fig.4.23 The Network Setup Wizard starts with the usual Welcome page

The initial page (Figure 4.23) simply gives a brief explanation of what the Network Setup Wizard will do. The next page (Figure 4.24) provides an opportunity to obtain background information from the Help system. It also explains that everything in the network must be fully installed, connected together, switched on, and ready to use. The wizard will not help with such things as setting up an Internet connection or installing device drivers for Ethernet or wi-fi cards. It just sets up the network once installation has been completed.

On the next page (Figure 4.25) the setup process starts, and the wizard has detected a shared Internet connection. This is actually provided by a combined access point, router, and ADSL modem. A different Internet connection can be selected or the existing one can be used. In this case there is no alternative available, and the existing Internet connection has to be used. On the following page (Figure 4.26) the computer is given the name that will be used for it on the network, and a brief description can also be added here.

The network (workgroup) name is provided at the next page (Figure 4.27), or you can simply settle for the default name (MSHOME). This completes the setting up process, and a page that shows the selected

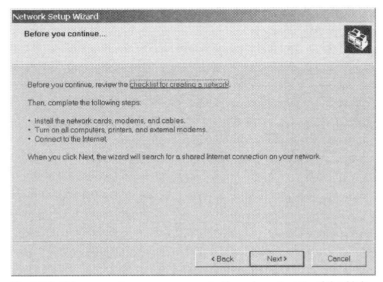

Fig.4.24 This page gives easy access to the relevant parts of the Help system

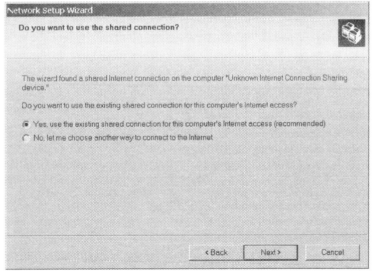

Fig.4.25 The wizard has detected a shared Internet connection

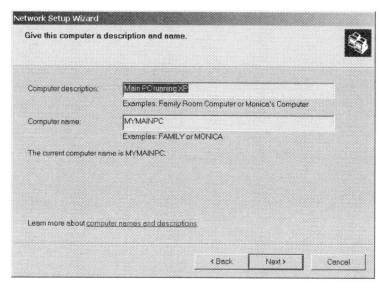

Fig.4.26 Use this page to name the computer and provide a
brief description

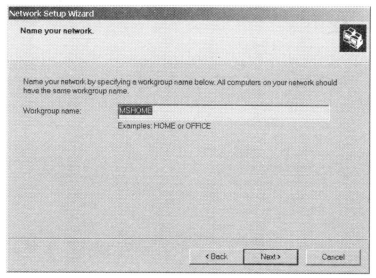

Fig.4.27 Here the name for the workgroup is entered in the textbox

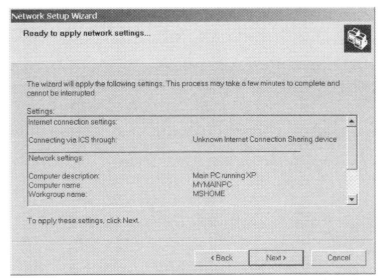

Fig.4.28 This window enables the selected settings to be reviewed

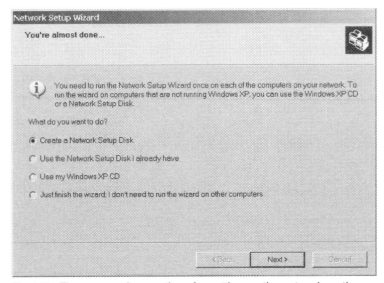

*Fig.4.29 There are various options for setting up the network on the
other PCs in the system*

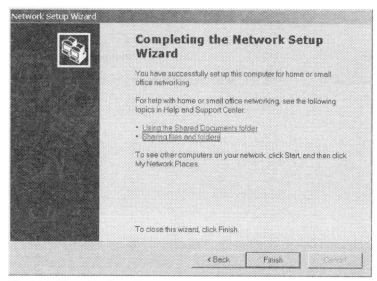

Fig.4.30 The wizard confirms that the process has been completed

settings is displayed (Figure 4.28) when the Next button is operated. Windows then does some reconfiguring of itself before displaying the page shown in Figure 4.29. This gives various options for setting up networking on the other PCs in the system. You can simply exit the wizard if the other PCs in the network are running Windows ME and/or XP, and then run the Network Setup Wizard in the usual way on those PCs. Finally, the page shown in Figure 4.30 confirms that the process has been completed.

Sharing folders

A network is only worthwhile if some resources are shared, but it is not essential to have shared resources on every computer in the network. In order to share the resources of a computer it is necessary to have the appropriate type of sharing enabled. With Windows ME it is possible to disable sharing, and in the interests of good security it is advisable not to enable sharing unless it will be used on the PC in question. Note that it is not necessary to have sharing enabled in order to use a PC to access resources on other PCs. Any PC in the system can be used to access

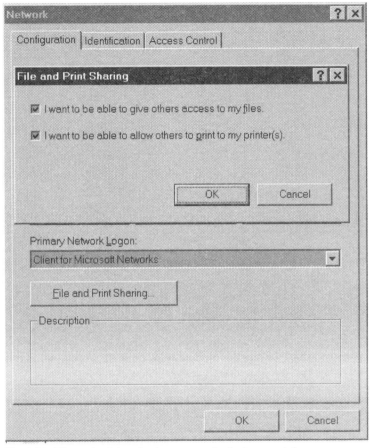

Fig.4.31 File and printer sharing are controlled separately

shared resources on other PCs. You only have to enable sharing on a PC that will make resources available to the network.

To enable or disable sharing in Windows ME it is first necessary to go to the Windows Control Panel and double-click the Network icon. Left-click the Configuration tab and then operate the File and Print Sharing button. This launches a small window (Figure 4.31) where two checkboxes provide individual control over file and printer sharing. Operate the OK button when the required changes have been made, and then the OK button on the Network window.

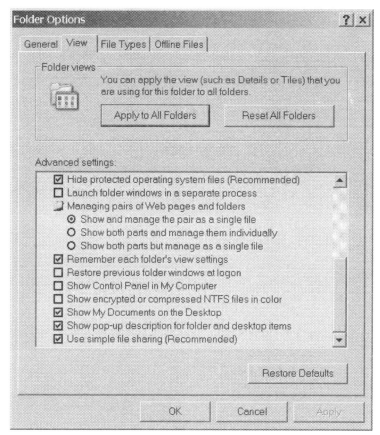

Fig.4.32 The "Use simple file sharing" option is suitable for most users

Windows XP Home has a new system of file sharing called "simple file sharing", and this is the default setting for Windows XP Professional. Simple file sharing can be turned off in Windows XP Professional by double-clicking the My Computer icon on the desktop, and selecting Folder Options from the Tools menu. Left-click the View tab and then scroll down the list in the main part of the window until you find the entry that reads "Use simple file sharing (Recommended)" (Figure 4.32). Remove the tick from its checkbox and then operate the Apply and OK buttons. For most purposes the default setting will suffice, and it is assumed here that the simple file sharing method is used.

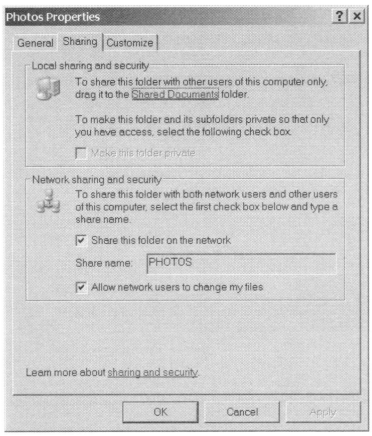

Fig.4.33 Use this window to enable sharing of a folder

In order to share a folder, first locate it using Windows Explorer, and then right-click on its entry. From the pop-up menu select Properties, and then operate the Sharing tab in the properties window (Figure 4.33). Place a tick in the "Share this folder on the network" checkbox in order to make the folder available to the network. By default, the contents of the folder can be read via the network, but they can not be altered. Full access to the folder can be provided by ticking the "Allow network users to change my files" checkbox. The folder can be shared under its normal name, or a different name can be typed into the Shared name textbox.

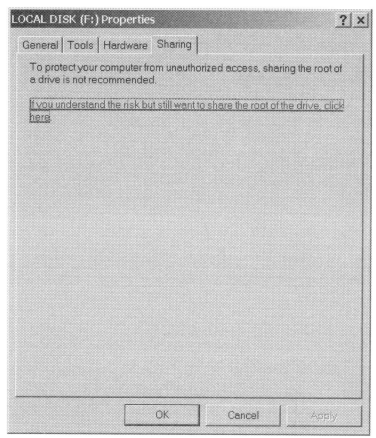

Fig.4.34 This warning message appears if you try to share a disc

Operate the Apply and OK buttons to exit the window and make the changes take effect.

Essentially the same method is used to share a complete disc. However, on entering the Sharing section of the disc's Properties window you obtain a warning message (Figure 4.34). If you wish to continue anyway, left-click the link text and the properties window will then change to the normal sharing type. It can then be shared in the same way as a folder (Figure 4.35), but in most circumstances this method of sharing is definitely not a good idea.

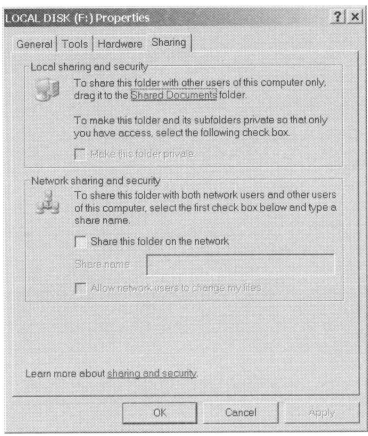

Fig.4.35 A disc can be shared, if you are prepared to accept the risks

Network Places

Having shared a disc or folder, the shared resource can then be added to the Network Places of any PC that will need to access it. Start by double-clicking the My Network Places icon on the desktop. The PC used for this example already has a couple of network places added (Figure 4.36), but when starting "from scratch" the right-hand section of the My Network Places window will be blank. Left-click "Add a network place" in the upper left-hand section of the window, which will launch a

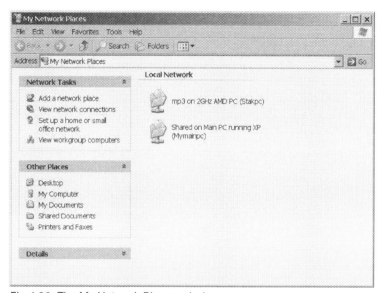

Fig.4.36 The My Network Places window

Fig.4.37 The Welcome screen for the Network Places Wizard

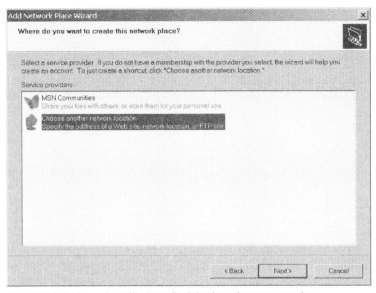

Fig.4.38 Windows is unlikely to find the location you require

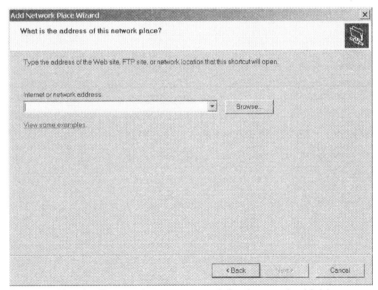

Fig.4.39 Use the Browse button to search for the required folder

new window (Figure 4.37). This is just a Welcome screen, so operate the Next button to move on to the window of Figure 4.38.

Windows will search for new network places, but it will not find very much. Consequently, you have to choose the option that lets you specify a network location. This moves things on to the window of Figure 4.39, where it is advisable to operate

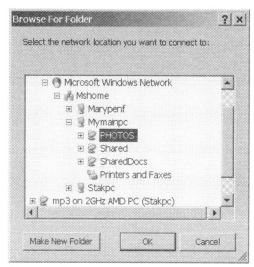

Fig.4.40 The required folder has been found

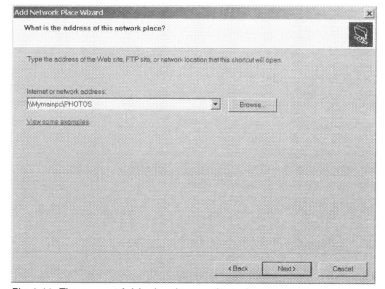

Fig.4.41 The correct folder has been selected

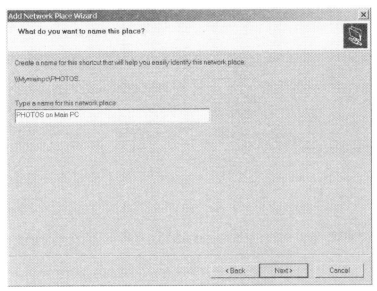

Fig.4.42 A name for the network place can be provided here

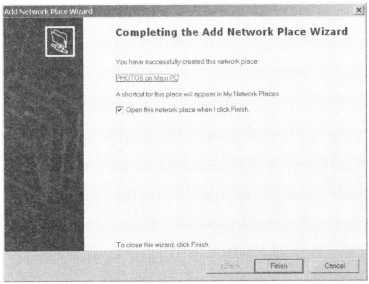

Fig.4.43 This window confirms that the process has been completed

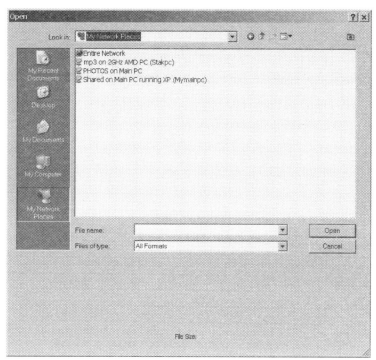

Fig.4.44 The shared folder is available in file browsers

the Browse button and then use the file browser to search for the new network place. The browser provides access to all available parts of the network, and the required PHOTOS folder on Mymainpc was easily located (Figure 4.40). Having selected the correct folder, operate the OK button and the network address will be added to the textbox in the main window (Figure 4.41).

A name for the new network place can be added in the textbox at the next window (Figure 4.42), or you can settle for the suggested default name. The next window (Figure 4.43) simply informs you that the task has been completed. Tick the checkbox if you wish to open the newly added folder in Windows Explorer when the Finish button is operated.

The new network place can be easily accessed using Windows Explorer or the standard Windows file browser built into most applications

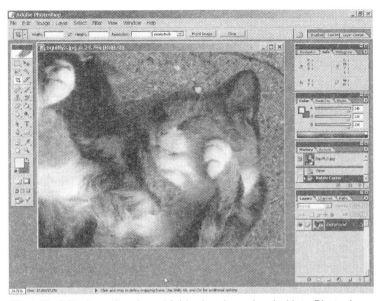

Fig.4.45 A file from the shared folder has been loaded into Photoshop

programs. As one would expect, it will be found in the My Network Places folder, together with any other network places that are installed. In Figure 4.44 the PHOTOS folder has been located in the file browser of Photoshop CS. It can be opened in the usual way, and then a file can be loaded (Figure 4.45).

Note that it will only be possible to read files unless you opted to permit changes to files when setting the sharing options for the folder. If changes are permitted, it is then possible to change files in an applications program and save the changes in the usual way. Where permission to alter files has not been given, it is still possible to load and edit them. The edited files must be saved to another folder though, so that the original files are left untouched.

Printer sharing

Ideally a printer should be shared via a printer server so that it is always available to any PC in the network. As printer servers are not particularly cheap, most users opt for the alternative of sharing a printer that is connected to a PC in the normal way. Windows has built-in sharing

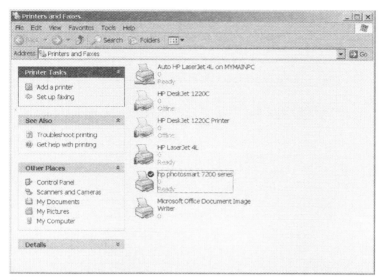

Fig.4.46 The Printers and Faxes window

facilities to handle this, but it requires rather more setting up than sharing folders or a disc. Bear in mind that a printer shared in this way can not be used when the PC that drives it is switched off. This can mean having to switch on a PC simply to permit a printer to be used via the network.

The first task is to determine whether the printer you wish to share has sharing enabled. Go to the PC to which the printer is directly connected, launch the Windows Control Panel, and then double-click the Printers and Faxes icon. This will produce a window something like Figure 4.46, but its exact appearance will depend on the particular printers and faxes that are installed on the computer. Any printers that have sharing enabled will have a picture of a hand included in their icons.

In this example an HP Photosmart 7200 series printer will be shared, and as things stand, it is not set for shared operation. To enable sharing, right-click the printer's icon and select Sharing from the pop-up menu. In the new window that appears (Figure 4.47), operate the "Share this printer" radio button, and add a name for the printer in the textbox.

At this stage you can operate the Apply and OK buttons if all the PCs in the network use the same operating system. Matters are complicated slightly if you will need to use the printer with a PC that has a different operating system to the one that is normally used with the printer. A

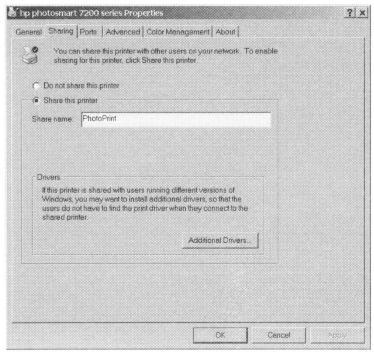

*Fig.4.47   Sharing is enabled using the appropriate radio button and a
name for the printer is then added in the textbox*

different operating system will almost certainly require a different set of
device drivers. Where appropriate, these drivers must be installed before
proceeding.

Operating the Additional Drivers button produces a small window, similar
to the one shown in Figure 4.48. This lists all the available device drivers
for the printer, and there is a tick in the checkbox for those that are already
installed. Tick the boxes for any more that need to be installed, and then
operate the OK button. The window of Figure 4.49 then appears, and
you have to direct the installation program to the source for the drivers.
This will usually be the CD-ROM provided with the printer, or files
downloaded from the Internet. Anyway, the usual installation process is
then followed, and you should eventually arrive back at the Printers and
Faxes window, which will show that the printer is set up for sharing (Figure
4.50).

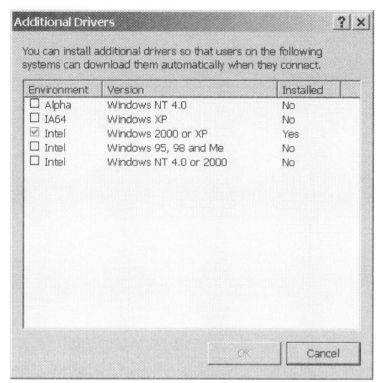

Fig.4.48 A list of the supported operating systems is displayed

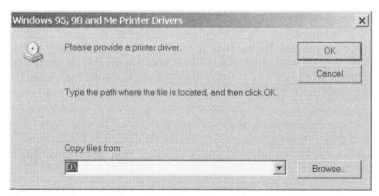

Fig.4.49 Indicate the location of the drivers when this window appears

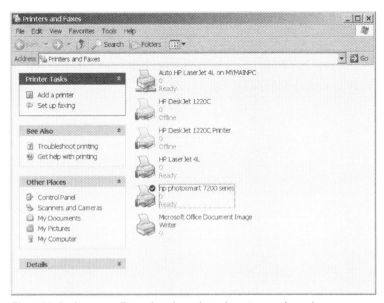

*Fig.4.50 Its icon confirms that the printer is set as a shared
resource*

Printer installation

Before a shared printer can be used on another PC, it must be installed
on that PC. The installation process for a networked printer is different
to that for a local printer (one driven direct from the PC). Start the process
by going to the Printers and Faxes window in the PC that is accessing
the printer via the network. This has icons for the currently installed
printers and faxes, with no icon at this stage for the Photosmart printer
(Figure 4.51).

Start the installation process by operating the Add Printer link near the
top left-hand corner of the window. This launches the Add Printer Wizard,
and the first page is, as usual, the Welcome screen (Figure 4.52). At the
next page (Figure 4.53) there is the option of installing a local or network
printer, and in this case it is clearly the radio button for a network printer
that is used.

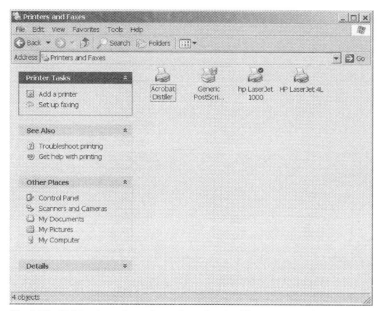

Fig.4.51 At this stage there is no icon for the Photosmart printer

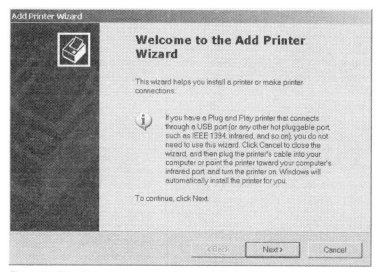

Fig.4.52 The Welcome screen of the Add Printer Wizard

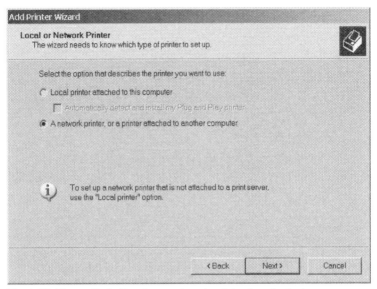

Fig.4.53 The radio button for a network printer is selected

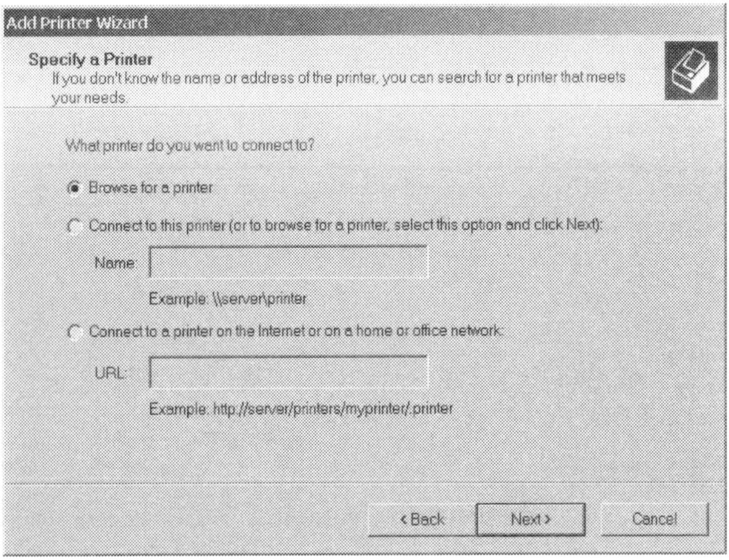

Fig.4.54 Specify a printer or use the browse option

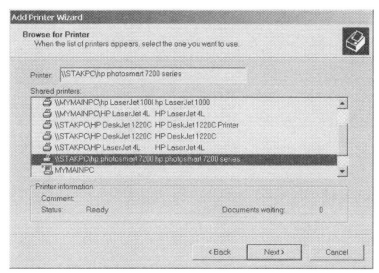

Fig.4.55 The correct printer has been found by using the browser

It is then necessary to indicate the printer you wish to install, and it is advisable to use the browse option here (Figure 4.54). Having located the correct printer using the browser (Figure 4.55), operate the Next button. A standard virus warning screen will then appear (Figure 4.56), but there will presumably be no risk in downloading a driver from one of your own PCs. Finally, left-click the Yes button to go ahead and install the device drivers for the printer. There is no need to have the drivers disc for the printer, because the drivers will be obtained from the network PC that already has them installed. Note that an error message will be produced if this PC does not have the device drivers for the correct operating system.

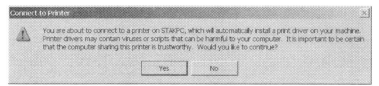

Fig.4.56 It should be safe to ignore the standard virus warning

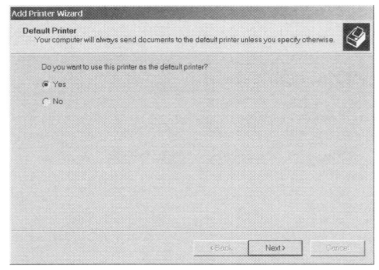

Fig.4.57 The printer can be the default unit if desired

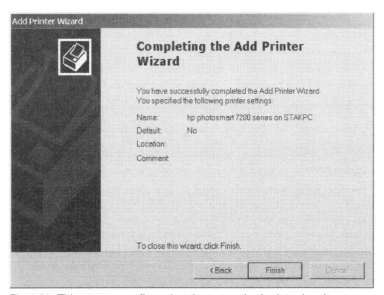

Fig.4.58 This screen confirms that the networked printer has been
          successfully installed

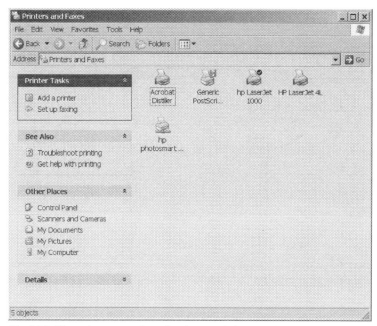

Fig.4.59 There is now an icon for the newly installed printer

To complete the installation you must decide whether the newly installed printer should be set as the default type (Figure 4.57). In other words, should it be set as the printer that will be used unless Windows is instructed otherwise? Finally, the page of Figure 4.58 informs you that the installation has been completed successfully. It is advisable to go back to the Printers and Faxes window to ensure that an icon for the newly installed printer is present and correct. In this case everything has gone to plan and the icon is present (Figure 4.59).

The printer can then be used in much the same way as if it was a local printer. Of course, it can only be used when the PC it is connected to is actually switched on. Less obviously, it is likely that "Out of paper", "Low ink", and similar status or error messages will appear on the screen of the PC that drives the printer. This is not very convenient if you are using a printer that is in a different room on another floor of the building, but you just have to learn to live with this limitation.

The newly networked printer should be listed when you try to print from an application program (Figure 4.60). Having selected the printer it should

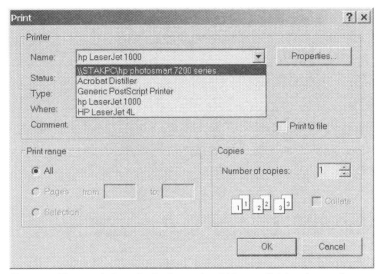

*Fig.4.60   The newly installed printer should be available when using
any Windows application that has a Print facility*

then be possible to launch its properties window (Figure 4.61) so that
the paper type, print quality, etc., can be selected. The amount of data
sent to a printer can be massive, so results are likely to be obtained
more quickly using an 802.11g or wired network connection. Printing
can be noticeably slower when using a poor quality 802.11b link.

Internet sharing

Internet sharing works best with a fast connection that is always on. With
a slow dialup Internet connection it will probably not be worthwhile sharing
a connection. In theory it enables all users to access the Internet at any
time, but in practice the Internet connection will probably not be left
permanently switched on. Because voice and Internet calls can not be
handled simultaneously, a connection to the Internet is normally made
only when it is actually needed.

Another factor to bear in mind is that sharing a 56k Internet connection
provides each user with very little bandwidth. If one user decides to
download a large file, the other users could find that their Internet access
is effectively blocked. Each PC having its own modem is in many ways
a more practical solution. Users have to take it in turn to access the

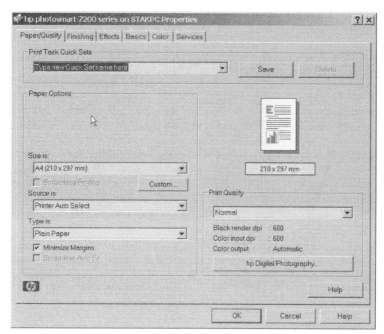

Fig.4.61 The Properties window can be accessed in the usual way

Internet, but they do at least have a reasonable connection speed while they are online.

There is a minimal speed problem when sharing a broadband Internet connection. With (say) an ordinary 512k ADSL connection, even with four or five users, each person would have an effective bandwidth of over 100k. This is still around double the speed of a 56k dialup connection.

The best way of sharing some form of broadband Internet connection is to use a router connected to a broadband modem, or a combined router and broadband modem. In a wi-fi context it is more likely that a combined access point, broadband modem, and router, or equivalent separate units, would be used. With this method the unit containing the modem is left turned on all the time, making an Internet connection permanently available to any PC in the system. There is no need to set up Internet sharing on any of the PCs in the network. With the equipment set up correctly and running, Windows will automatically find and use the Internet connection. The sharing process is not readily apparent to users, with each one appearing to have their own Internet connection.

Alternative method

Another way of implementing sharing of a broadband Internet connection is to have a broadband modem connected to one of the PCs in the network, and for the other PCs to access the Internet via this PC. There are two drawbacks to this method. One is simply that the Internet connection is dependent on the PC that is connected to the modem being operational. Switch off that PC, and all the other computers in the network lose their Internet connection. The other problem is that heavy use of the Internet could place a significant drain on the resources of the PC connected to the modem. Software is used to effectively turn the PC into a router.

Another point to bear in mind is that the PC connected to the modem, if fitted with a wi-fi adapter, does not become a wireless access point. It is just another PC in the network. The Internet connection is just another shared resource, much like a shared printer. Therefore, in order to wi-fi enable the network you will still require an access point.

This software method of sharing an Internet connection has little to recommend it, and I would never use it. The normal reason for using this method is to permit an existing USB modem to be used, rather than buying one with an Ethernet port or using a combined modem and router. With the current low cost of computer hardware, any small additional expense with the hardware method would seem to be well justified.

Anyway, if you should decide to use this method, Windows ME has an Internet Connection Sharing Wizard that makes the process as straightforward as possible. This is not usually installed as a standard part of Windows ME, so you will probably have to go to the Control Panel and double-click the Add-Remove Programs icon. Operate the Windows Setup tab and then highlight the entry for Internet Tools. Operate the Details button so that the individual tools are shown, and tick the box for Internet Sharing. Operate the OK buttons and the required wizard will be installed and run. The Windows installation disc is required to complete this task.

With Windows XP there is more than one way of tackling Internet connection sharing. Probably the easiest way is to set up the network in the appropriate fashion when running the Network Connection Wizard on each computer. The wizard can be run again in order to change the network's configuration if you did not opt for connection sharing when initially setting up the network.

Firmware upgrades

With the system "up and running" it is advisable to check the relevant manufacturer's web sites from time to time in case there are any driver or firmware updates. These are often needed in order to sort out minor problems that become apparent when the products are used in earnest by thousands of users. In some cases there are definite faults in the original software or firmware. Often the problems are more obscure, and typically they only occur when certain combinations of hardware or hardware and software are used.

Where a network is running well it is not necessarily a good idea to install firmware updates, but it is probably as well to install any improved drivers that are available. There is little risk involved in using updated drivers, and the Roll Back Driver feature of Windows XP makes it easy to return to the previous drivers if the new ones should prove to be problematic. The Roll Back Driver facility is accessed by going to the relevant entry in Device Manager, right-clicking it, selecting Properties from the pop-up window, and then operating the Driver tab in the Properties window. Then operate the Roll Back Driver button near the bottom of the window

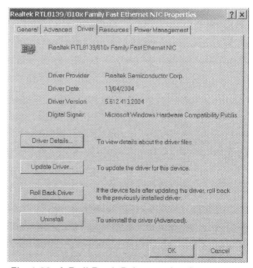

Fig.4.62 A Roll Back Driver option is available in Windows XP

(Figure 4.62). In theory, the Update Driver button in the same window is used when installing a newer driver. In practice it is more usual for the updated driver to be installed via its own installation program. Always follow the installation instructions provided by the manufacturer.

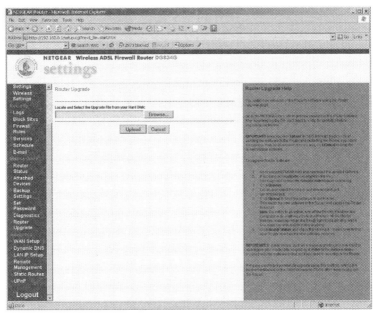

Fig.4.63 The DG834's control software includes an Upgrade section

It is advisable not to upgrade the firmware unless some real benefit will be gained in doing so. There is a slight risk involved when upgrading firmware. If the process should go wrong it is possible that the upgraded unit would be left unusable. It might then be necessary to return it to the maker to be repaired. The risk is actually very small. If you should happen to download the wrong data file, it is likely that the upgrade routine would spot the error and refuse to go ahead with the upgrade.

The main danger is that something will interrupt the process, resulting in the unit having a combination of old and new firmware. This is almost certain to leave it in an unusable state. You would have to be very unlucky indeed for a power cut to occur during the few seconds it takes to complete an upgrade. There is probably a greater risk of interrupting the upgrade by accidentally knocking a connector out of place or switching something off. During the upgrade, keep still and touch none of the equipment or wiring.

Note that with some units it is not possible to go back to an earlier version of the firmware. I am not sure why this should be the case, but where

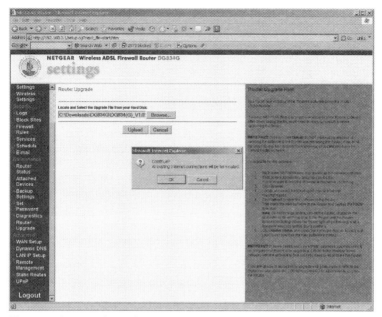

Fig.4.64 Operate the OK button when this warning message appears

there is no way back to the original version it would definitely not be a good idea to upgrade the firmware if the current version is working well. Upgrading would involve a slight risk of introducing bugs into a unit that previously worked flawlessly, with no way of going back to a fully working version of the firmware. It might be worth the slight risk if the new firmware has added features such as improved security options, but it is otherwise not worth the risk. It is definitely a case of "if it ain't broke, don't fix it".

If you find a firmware upgrade and decide to go ahead with it, there are two normal methods of upgrading firmware. The simpler of the two is where the downloaded file is an executable program that contains embedded data. A file of this type will have an exe extension, and will be categorised as an "Application" in Windows Explorer. With this type of upgrade you just run the program and it updates the firmware. You can use the Run option in the Start menu, but double-clicking its entry in Windows Explorer is easier.

The unit that is being upgraded will usually have to be connected to the PC in a direct manner. For example, a USB wi-fi adapter would probably have to be upgraded via its USB interface and not by way of a wi-fi link from another PC in the system. With something like an access point it might be necessary to use a wired (Ethernet) connection rather than a wi-fi link. Always read the "fine print" before carrying out a firmware upgrade, and make sure that everything is being done in accordance with the manufacturer's recommendations.

With the second method of upgrading, the file you download is the data for the flash memory in the device that is being upgraded. A program is needed in order to program the data into whatever you are upgrading. A suitable program might have been supplied with the equipment, or it might be available as a download. It is also possible that the configuration software supplied with the unit has a facility for performing firmware upgrades. It is again a matter of finding the upgrade instructions and following them "to the letter".

In the case of the DG834G access point, the upgrade file I downloaded from the web site was a Zip file that had to be decompressed to extract its contents. A program such as WinZip is needed to do this, and programs such as this are widely available on the Internet. The extracted files were instructions in the form of an Adobe PDF file, and the image file containing the new data. The DG834G's web-based configuration program is used to perform the upgrade, and it has a Router Upgrade section specifically for this purpose (Figure 4.63).

The upgrade is performed by operating the Browse button, and then using the file browser to locate and select the appropriate file. It is unlikely that the program will go ahead with the upgrade if the wrong file is selected, but it would be as well to avoid errors just in case. With the right file selected, it just a matter of operating the Upload button, followed by the OK button when a warning message appears (Figure 4.64). This message just points out that all Internet connections will be terminated so that the upgrade can proceed. Writing to flash memory can be quite slow, so it might take a minute or two for the upload to be completed. The upgraded device is then ready to be put back into service again.

Points to remember

Read the manufacturer's installation guide before installing any new hardware. It can be time consuming to sort things out if you get the installation of the device drivers wrong. Before installing any supporting software it is advisable to check the manufacturer's web site for updated drivers, support software, and firmware.

The easy way of setting up a PC to operate with networking is to run the Windows Network Setup Wizard on each PC in the system. However, once this has set up the PCs to use networking, there is still some work to do in order to implement file and printer sharing across the network.

Each PC in the network is given a name so that it is easily located when using other PCs in the system. Make sure that each PC is given a different name. The network as a whole is also given a name.

Files and folders are easily shared using the built-in facilities of Windows XP or ME. By default, folders are not shared. Consequently, you must enable sharing for any folder that you wish to make available to the network. Then add the folder to the My Network Places of any PC that will use the folder.

It is possible to share an entire hard disc, but for security reasons it is not a good idea to do so if the network is connected to the Internet.

Any printer that is installed on a PC in the network can usually be shared and used by any other PC in the network. However, the printer can only be shared using a PC that is running an operating system for which a suitable printer driver is available. This should not be a problem if all the PCs are running a modern version of Windows, but Linux and other operating systems might not be supported.

The Internet connection of one PC can be shared with other PCs in the network, but this is an inefficient way of handling things. A modem connected to a router is a much better way of sharing an Internet connection, and these days it is unlikely to cost significantly more than the alternatives.

There is a very slight risk of rendering a unit unusable when upgrading its firmware. Unless a firmware upgrade will provide useful new features, it is probably not worthwhile upgrading a unit that functions perfectly. Always follow the manufacturer's upgrade instructions "to the letter".

Troubleshooting and optimising

Try it

It would be helpful if there was an easy way of working out whether a wi-fi link from point A to point B would work properly. Something close to the theoretical maximum operating range should be obtained if there are not too many major obstructions between the two aerials. By major obstructions I mean walls, ceilings, floors, central heating radiators, and substantial items of furniture. Objects outside the path between the aerials can cause problems by reflecting the signals, but you would be unlucky if this factor seriously shortened the range of the system.

Of course, in practice it is unlikely that there will be a clear path from the access point's aerial to any other aerial in the system. After all, one of the main reasons for using wi-fi equipment is to avoid having to take cables through walls, floors, etc. Walls, floors, ceilings, are the main causes of reduced range when wi-fi equipment is used indoors, but large items of furniture or any other substantial objects that get in the way will absorb some of the signal and reduce the operating range.

Large metal objects such as radiators go beyond absorbing some of the signal, and tend to block it completely. The metal framework of some buildings can give similar problems. It is possible that other items will act as reflectors to provide a path around metal objects, but this is unlikely to provide good results. It pays to bear in mind relatively small objects, if sufficiently close to an aerial, can significantly reduce the range of the system.

Ultimately there is only one way to determine whether a link can be successfully established between any two points in a building, and that is to try it and see. Provided the range is less than the theoretical indoor figure for the standard you are using, it should be possible to obtain a link. However, near the maximum range it might not be possible to obtain operation at maximum speed.

Of course, in situations where it is not possible to avoid having a large piece of metal between the two aerials it is probably not worth trying a wi-fi link. This is especially so if the link will be required to operate over anything more than a very modest range.

A wired connection is the more practical proposition in these circumstances. It will be more difficult to install, but at least it will actually work, and at a very high speed. Fortunately, in the real-world you are unlikely to encounter a metal obstacle large enough to block or severely attenuate a wi-fi signal.

Planning

The chances of problems occurring can be minimised by carefully planning the system, rather than just placing everything for maximum convenience. The most convenient place for the access point might be at one corner of the building, but this is the worst position in terms of performance. Any wi-fi devices on the other side of the building will be a long way from the access point. By positioning the access point near the middle of the building you ensure that no wi-fi enabled gadget can be much more than about half the width of the building from the access point.

In theory a range of up to about 20 metres can be obtained indoors when using 802.11g equipment, and the range is much higher at about 60 metres for 802.11b links. These are the maximum ranges for operation at top speed incidentally. Even assuming that these ranges will not quite be achieved in practice, an 802.11g link should still give full coverage in a building up to about 25 to 30 metres square. Obviously the access point must be close to the centre of the building in order to achieve this level of coverage.

This should be adequate for most purposes, but accepting the lower speed of an 802.11b link gives much greater range. A building of around 80 to 100 metres square should be within the capabilities of a well designed 802.11b system. Remember that the 802.11b and 802.11g standards are compatible. It is therefore possible to use an 802.11g access point with 802.11g adapters for PCs that are close to the access point, and 802.11b adapters for those that are further away. This gives high-speed transfers for the PCs that are close to the access point, but retains the longer range needed for those that are further away.

Simple problems

It would be unrealistic to expect a perfect signal every time when installing wi-fi equipment. The performance of wi-fi links is not totally predictable, you might make a mistake when installing and setting up the system, or if you are very unlucky a component in the network could be faulty. When troubleshooting on any computer equipment it is essential to go about things in a logical fashion and to avoid jumping to conclusions. Do not immediately assume that a lack of signal is due to range problems, especially when there is no signal at all. There could indeed be a problem with the range of the link being inadequate, but it could just be that there is some simple problem with the equipment.

Is everything plugged in and connected properly? When installing new equipment it is easy to get impatient and rush things. This is usually a mistake and it invites problems with things not being plugged in, switched on, or set up correctly. When hastily installing equipment it is easy to knock one lead out of place while installing another. Systematically check that everything is connected properly, switched on, and that the settings are correct. Make sure that everything is working on the same channel.

It seems to be a feature of networking equipment that it sometimes "loses the plot".   Actually, it is not unknown for this to happen with wired networks. The standard solution is to switch everything off and then power-up the system again. Switch on the access point first, then any devices that use a wired network, and finally switch on the wi-fi units.

Moving experience

The UHF (ultra-high frequency) radio signals used by wi-fi equipment have very short wavelengths, and this can result in signal strengths varying considerably if one of the aerials is moved a small distance. Even moving an aerial a few centimetres can produce a significant change in signal strength. One reason for this is that quite small objects in the wrong place can partially block the signal. You might occasionally find that what was a very good signal suddenly becomes a noticeably weaker one. The most likely cause is that something placed closed to one of the aerials is absorbing the signal.

Another problem is due to reflected signals that combine with the main signal. It is possible that the two signals will combine in a fashion that produces a boost in signal, but it is just as likely that they will have a cancelling effect, giving a reduction in the signal level. In an extreme case there can be one or more "blind" spots where there is no significant signal. Again, something being moved to just the wrong place can produce a sudden decrease in the signal level.

The cure in both cases is to move the aerial in an attempt to obtain a better signal level. This should not be a problem with an external wi-fi interface that connects to the PC via a cable. With an interface mounted on some form of portable computer it might be a trifle inconvenient, but it should still be possible to move the device in an attempt to obtain a better signal. Moving the aerial is clearly going to be more difficult if it is fixed to a substantial piece of equipment such as a desktop PC or a printer. In this respect, PCI wi-fi adapters are very restrictive.

Rather than moving the entire PC and (possibly) redesigning your office to get the wi-fi link to work well, it would probably be better to get an extension cable to permit the aerial to be positioned away from the PC. Having the aerial right next to the earthed metal case of the PC is far from ideal. Despite your best efforts it may well be in amongst some

cables as well (Figure 5.1), and these will make matters worse. The truth of the matter is that the rear of a PC is just about the worst place to have a wi-fi aerial. Moving the aerial away from the cables and the PC's case will often provide much improved results.

The problems are much the same with a USB wi-fi adapter that plugs straight into the back of the PC. A USB extension cable enables the unit to be used away from the

Fig.5.1   The aerial is in there somewhere!

PC and will often give much better results. Note that this does not require the usual A to B lead of the type used with printers, scanners, and most other USB peripherals. An A to A cable of the type used to link two PCs is not the right type either. These contain some electronics and are quite

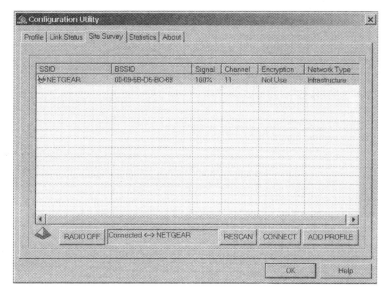

Fig.5.2 This section only gives the signal strength via a text entry

expensive. It is a simple and inexpensive A to A extension cable that is needed.

Signal strength

It is clearly more than a little helpful to have some form of signal strength monitor so that you can see how changes in the positions of the aerial affect reception. Without the aid of a signal strength monitor there is little chance of adjusting a link for optimum results. The software supplied with a wi-fi adapter usually includes a utility that shows the available access points, together with some information about each one. This should include the names of the networks, the channels they are occupying, and the signal strength of each one.

Some form of graphic indication of signal strength is best, since it enables the reading to be seen at a glance. Many wi-fi adapters are supplied with software that includes a bargraph, or something similar, to indicate the signal strength. A few either lack any form of signal strength meter or provide a reading via a text display. Figure 5.2 shows the monitor program for a cheap generic 802.11b PCI card. This is better than nothing

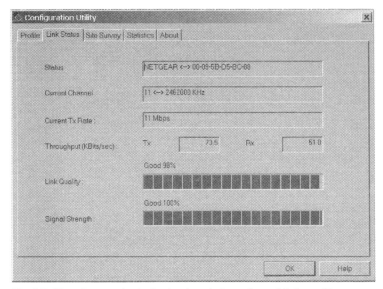

Fig.5.3 Here bargraphs indicate signal-strength and link quality

in that it does provide a signal strength reading, but it is in the form of a text entry that gives a reading from 0 to 100 percent.

Fortunately, in this case another section of the program (Figure 5.3) has two bargraphs that show the quality of the link and the signal strength, so it pays to check through all the facilities offered by the support software. It might seem unnecessary to have indications of both signal strength and link quality, but good signal strength does not guarantee a high quality link. A lot of electrical noise or interference from another wi-fi system can result in poor results despite excellent signal strength.

There are programs available that provide a signal strength meter, and probably the best know free program of this type is Boingo, which can be downloaded from:

http://www.boingo.com/download.html

This is actually intended as an aid to finding and connecting to wireless hotspots, but it has a graphic signal strength indicator for each access point that is located. In Figure 5.4 just the one access point has been

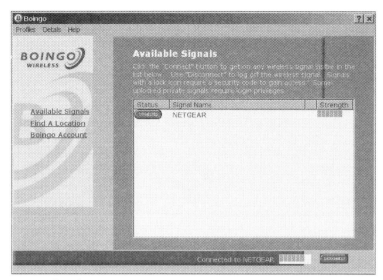

Fig.5.4 The Boingo program has a small signal-strength bargraph

found, and the bargraph strength meter shows that a strong signal is being received. This program will not work with all wi-fi adapter cards, and the Boingo web site lists the compatible cards. It worked fine when I tried it with a cheap generic card, so it is probably worth trying the program even if your card is not listed. After all, it costs nothing to try the program and it is easily uninstalled if it fails to work with your wi-fi card.

When using a signal strength indicator it is as well to bear in mind that most of them do not update the display very frequently. Consequently, it might seem as though a change in the position of an aerial has had no effect, when the lack of response from the program is simply because it has not refreshed the display. After moving an aerial it is therefore necessary to wait a few seconds to see if there is any change to the indicated signal strength.

Access point

It can sometimes happen that poor results are obtained from all the wi-fi units in the system, even those that seem to be well positioned for good results. The most likely cause of this is the access point and its aerial being placed where nearby obstructions are absorbing much of the signal. Moving it to a different location might give greatly improved results.

Although the space between a PC and a monitor or printer will often be the most convenient place for the access point, having the aerial in amongst large electronic devices is likely to give poor results. The earthed metal case of a PC is likely to block the signal to and from large parts of the building. Results are likely to be better with the access point on top of the PC or positioned a metre or two away from it.

It is advisable not to have the aerial right next to a wall. Placing the access point on the floor is unlikely to give optimum results either. Hiding it out of sight inside a cupboard is almost certain to give a significant reduction in performance. Positioning the access point on a table or desk where it is not very close to walls, PCs, monitors, etc., is likely to give the best results.

Of course, the positioning of the access point is less critical if the system is only required to operate over short distances. It is then likely that acceptable results would indeed be obtained with it placed in a cupboard, between two large tower PCs, or whatever. The greater the range you are trying to achieve, the more carefully the aerials have to be positioned, with particular care being taken over the positioning of the access point. If the access point does not operate efficiently, the performance of the whole system will suffer.

Change channel

In theory it does not matter which channel you use for your wi-fi network. The small change in frequency from one channel to the next should have no significant effect on results. In practice, a change in channel will often produce greatly improved results from a network that is underperforming. Although one channel has no technical advantage over any other channel, in a real-world situation some will usually work much better than others.

The differences in performance are almost certainly due to some channels containing more noise than others do. Another wi-fi network some distance away might not produce a resolvable signal, but it could still cause significant interference across several channels. This interference will be too weak to give problems at short ranges, but at long ranges the signal levels drop and the system becomes much more susceptible to interference from other systems.

Wi-fi adapters are usually supplied with a program which lists the access points that are detected. In most cases your access point will be the only one that is listed, but inevitably some users will find that a few of their neighbours have wi-fi systems, and that these are listed as well. Try looking for access points with your own unit switched off. This will prevent it from blotting out signals from nearby systems, and increase the chances of detecting any that are present.

Clearly neither party will obtain really good results if the same channel is used for two systems. Less obviously, using adjacent channels will not improve matters very much, since wi-fi signals spread across several channels. If there are one or two other wi-fi systems in the area, use a channel that is as far removed as possible from the channel or channels that are currently in use. Some negotiation with your neighbours might be needed in order to get everyone using well separated channels.

Of course, equipment other than the wi-fi variety uses the 2.4GHz band, and it is possible that shorter than expected range is due to interference from one of these devices. Again, a change in channel might cure the problem. Moving up or down by one channel is unlikely to make much difference, because wi-fi and many other devices spread signals across several channels. A shift of about half a dozen channels is more likely to give an improvement. If necessary, try them all in order to find the one that gives optimum results. In order to change the channel used by the network it is first a matter of changing the channel used by the access point. The other units are then made to scan the band and find the access point again.

Most electronic gadgets generate electrical noise that covers a wide range of frequencies. The high operating frequency of wi-fi equipment means that it operates in a range that is well clear of most general radio noise, which is predominantly at frequencies below 100MHz. However, some gadgets produce a significant signal at frequencies of more than a gigahertz. Having the access point close to a microwave oven is not a good idea, and it is probably best not to have it right next to a monitor.

Boosting range

After a lot of repositioning of aerials and the access point it might become clear that the system is basically working, but the local terrain is such that one or two of the links will not work at maximum speed. This is unlikely to happen where the system is working comfortably within the theoretical range, but is clearly a possibility if you are trying to operate links near or beyond the normal limits. There are wi-fi options available in these circumstances, and the simplest one is to try using a directional aerial that provides gain. Wi-fi aerials offering high gains do not seem to be available, and they might fall outside the regulations governing the

2.4GHz band, so do not expect this method to provide a massive improvement.

Another option is to use one of the repeater units that are designed to be used between the access point and the remote unit. These can substantially extend the range of a system, but there is a significant additional cost involved in using a repeater, and finding a suitable unit could prove difficult. Before buying one it is essential to ensure that it will work with the rest of you system. Also, these units operate by receiving packets of data and then retransmitting them on the same channel. This inability to send and receive simultaneously tends to slow things down. Consequently, the performance of the link might not be vastly better than that of the unaided version.

A third option is to use two access points. This is normally done by having the two units linked by a wired connection, and having them operate on different channels at opposite ends of the band in order to minimise interference between what are really two linked but otherwise separate wi-fi networks. One obvious drawback is that it is not a totally wi-fi solution since a cable is needed to link the two access points. Another obvious drawback is that it involves the substantial added cost of a second access point.

Being pragmatic about it, when an improved aerial is insufficient to provide a really good link, the best options are probably to just settle for a relatively slow link, or to use a wired link if speed is important. Remember that a slow link is perfectly adequate if it is only needed to share a broadband Internet connection. The other options involve significant added expense and provide what has to be regarded as something less than a perfect solution.

Now you see it

With any equipment you can get everything apparently installed and working nicely, only to find that some while later it ceases to function correctly. There could be a hardware fault of course, but in most cases it is just that a lead has become detached, or something of this type. Networks tend to have a number of external peripheral devices and connecting leads, making them vulnerable to basic problems such as detached leads, switches that get accidentally knocked to the off position, and so on.

Wi-fi networks might have fewer cables and external peripherals, but they are not usually devoid of them. Wi-fi networks have the added

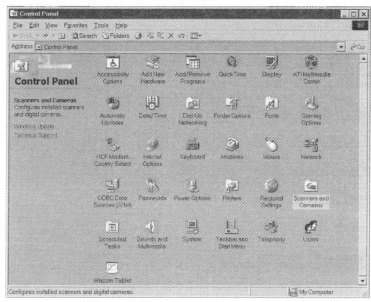

Fig.5.5 The Classic Windows ME version of Control Panel

vulnerability of aerials that can be knocked out of position or work loose. Check for basic faults first, rather than jumping to the conclusion that an item of hardware has become faulty. It is also worth checking that the supporting software is still installed correctly and fully working. The chances of this being the root of the trouble are much higher if any software has recently been installed or

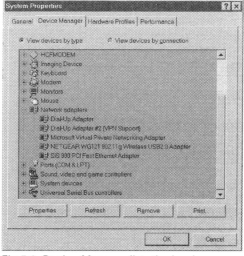

Fig.5.6 Device Manager lists the hardware

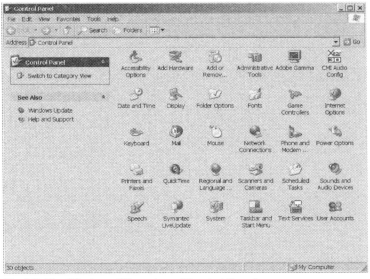

Fig.5.7 The Windows XP version of Control Panel

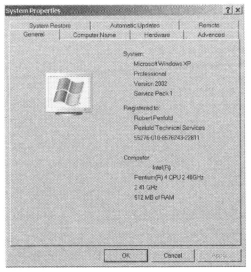

Fig.5.8 The System Properties window

uninstalled. It is probably worth uninstalling and reinstalling the software to see if this produces an improvement.

If a wi-fi link works well after installation, but does not function the next time you switch on the PC, there could be a hardware fault but it is more likely that the problem is in the software. After the a quick check for something simple such as a power lead that has come

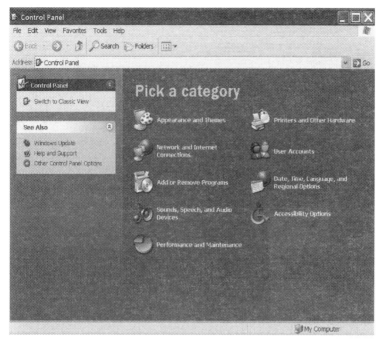

Fig.5.9 The Windows XP Control Panel in Category View

unplugged, the usual approach is to uninstall the hardware and then reinstall it from scratch.

It is not usually necessary to physically disconnect or remove any hardware from the PC. Uninstalling and reinstalling the drivers is usually sufficient. Having removed the drivers it is a good idea to shut down Windows and reboot the system before trying to reinstall the drivers. If you have not already checked the manufacturer's web site for updated drivers, it would definitely be a good idea to do so at this stage.

Removing drivers

In order to remove a device driver under Windows 98 and ME it is a matter of going into Device Manager, left-clicking on the relevant entry to highlight it and then operating the Remove button. In order to access

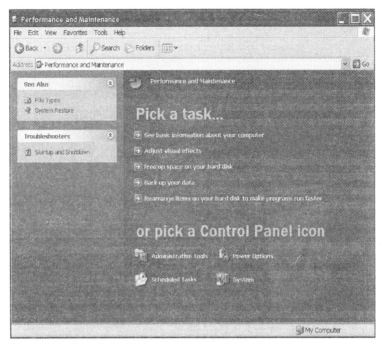

Fig.5.10 Left-click the System icon when this window appears

Device Manager, first select Settings from the Start menu, followed by Control Panel from the submenu that appears. The exact appearance of the Control Panel will depend on the setup of your PC, but it will probably look something like Figure 5.5. Double-click the System icon or text entry to launch the System Properties window, and then operate the Device Manager tab. The entry for a wi-fi adapter will normally be found in the Network Adapters section of Device Manager (Figure 5.6).

Device drivers are easily removed using the Windows XP version of Device Manager, but the process is rather different due to the lack of a Remove button. Also, the route to Device Manager is different. With the "Classic" version of the Control Panel (Figure 5.7), it is again a matter of double-clicking the system icon in order to produce the Windows XP version of the System Properties window (Figure 5.8). With the Category View selected (Figure 5.9), first select the Performance and Maintenance option near the bottom of the window, and then click the System icon in the

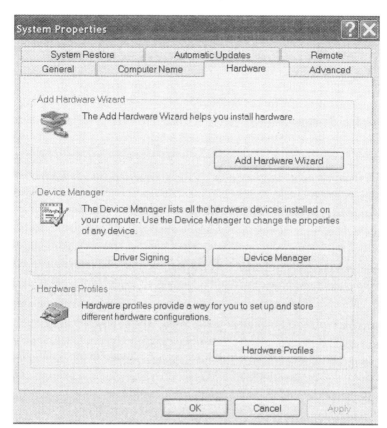

Fig.5.11 Operate the Device Manager button in the middle section of this window

new version of the window that appears (Figure 5.10). Once the System Properties window is on the screen, select the Hardware tab, which will change the window to look like Figure 5.11. Finally, operate the Device Manager button near the middle of the window.

As with Windows ME, wi-fi adapters are normally in the Network Adapters section (Figure 5.12). Right-clicking the wi-fi adapter's entry will produce a small popup menu (Figure 5.13), where the Uninstall option is selected. Essentially the same facilities can be obtained by double-clicking on the entry in Device Manager. This produces the property window for the

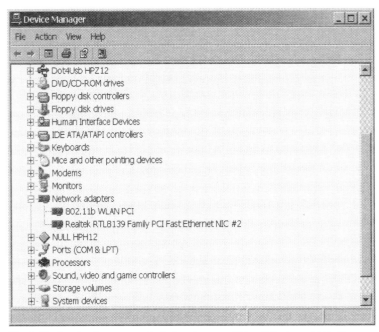

Fig.5.12 Again, the computer's hardware will be listed, and it is the Network adapters section that is of interest

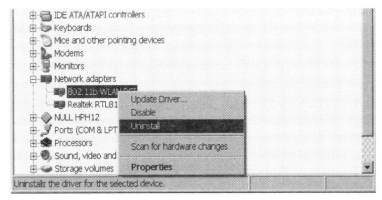

Fig.5.13 Right-clicking an entry produces a pop-up menu where an Uninstall option is available

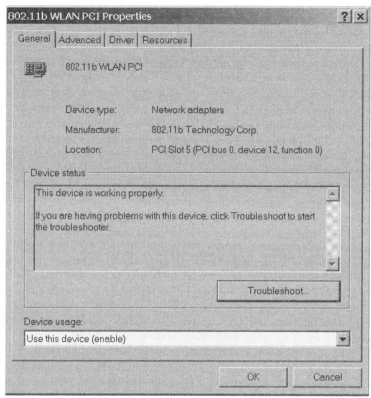

Fig.5.14 Each device has its own property window

device (Figure 5.14), and selecting the Driver tab switches the window to look something like Figure 5.15.

The Uninstall option is equivalent to the Remove button in Windows 9x, and it is used to remove the device driver. Note that with Plug and Play devices the drivers can only be uninstalled if the hardware is present in the PC and active. With the hardware absent or disabled, it will not have an entry in Device Manager. A warning message like the one in Figure 5.16 appears when the Uninstall button is operated. Left-click the Yes button in order to proceed and uninstall the device drivers. The entry for the uninstalled device should then disappear from the list in Device Manager.

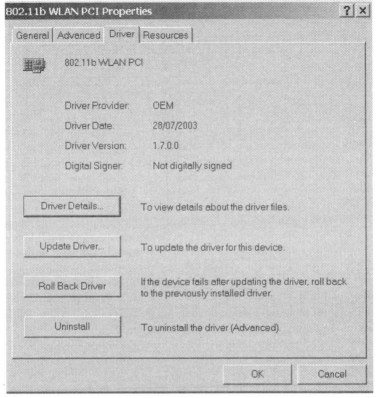

Fig.5.15 The Driver section includes an Uninstall button

Reinstalling

With the drivers uninstalled and the PC rebooted, the installation process can be repeated. In theory, installing the drivers should be no more successful at the second or third attempt than it was the first time. In practice it is often the case that one or two extra attempts provides a cure and gets the hardware working. Check the installation manual and make sure that you go through the installation process correctly.

In cases where following the manufacturer's instructions does not have the desired effect, it might be worth trying a different approach. For example, if installing the hardware first and then the software does not

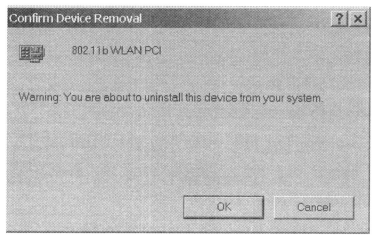

Fig.5.16 Operating the Uninstall button produces a warning message

get the everything working properly, try installing the software first and then the hardware. Some installation instructions do not match up with the supplied software, and generic devices are particularly prone to this problem.

A common problem is that Windows can not automatically detect the drivers, and it does not find them even if you direct it to the appropriate folder. The usual cause is that the folder does not contain the information file that Windows requires, or even the driver files as such. Examining the contents of the folder using Windows Explorer will often show that it contains an executable program file (one having an exe extension). There might also be a file that contains the real installation instructions. When trying to install problematic hardware it is worth searching the installation disc for a text or Adobe PDF file that contains more up-to-date installation instructions. Text and PDF files respectively have txt and pdf extensions.

Sometimes the executable file is a self-extracting archive. Doubling-clicking its entry in Windows Explorer will run the file, and a program embedded within it will then decompress the files and place them in the folder that you select. Windows should then be able to install the hardware if you direct it to that folder during the installation process. More usually, running the program file results in the drivers being automatically installed on the hard disc drive. You then have to reboot the PC so that Windows can complete the installation process. A further reboot might then be required in order to make the hardware fully operational.

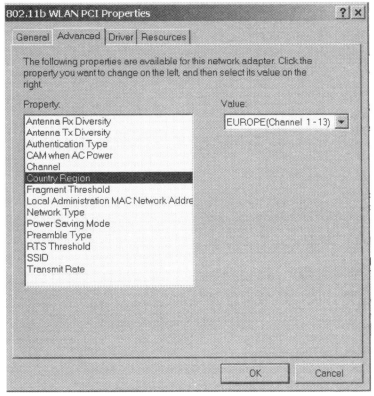

*Fig.5.17 A number of settings might be available from the device's
          properties window*

Country setting

When installing wi-fi equipment it is normal for the user to specify the
country in which the equipment will be used. This step is included when
installing many pieces of software, and it is normally done simply to
ensure that menus, etc., use the appropriate language. It has this function
when installing the support software for wi-fi equipment, but it also sets
up the hardware so that it operates with the appropriate parameters for
the country in which the equipment is being used. Although the two
radio bands used for wi-fi equipment are the same for all countries, the
regulations are different for each country. For instance, the channelling
operates differently from one country to another.

This makes it very important to select the right country when installing wi-fi equipment. Making a mistake here could result in the equipment operating in an illegal fashion, and it might not work properly with equipment that is set up correctly. Note that when installing many programs there is no UK English option, so the US English option has to be used. The US option must not be used when installing wi-fi equipment in the UK. There should either be a UK option or one called something like "Europe Channels 1 – 13". This is the option that must be used.

It is worth checking the main settings of any adapter that gives problems. There might be a control program, but it is common to have the settings controlled via an extension of the normal Windows facilities. To access the control software it is first a matter of right-clicking the adapter's entry in Device Manager. Then the Properties option is selected from the pop-up menu. The Properties window should have a section called something like Settings or Advanced, which enables parameters such as the default channel and country setting to be altered. Figure 5.17 shows the Advanced section for the Properties window for a generic PCI 802.11b adapter.

It is not a good idea to "play" with settings you do not understand, but the country setting can be checked, and corrected if it is wrong. It is a good idea to check that the default channel matches that used by the access point. Using the wrong channel is unlikely to prevent the adapter from communicating with the access point, because the control software usually scans for signals. It should therefore locate the default access point and join the network. However, having the correct default channel should reduce the risk of problems with the adapter struggling to find the access point.

Repairing a connection

It does sometimes happen that a unit in the network loses its network connection and has difficulty re-establishing contact. This can be due to the system "losing the plot" rather than any physical problem. If there is a physical problem such as a detached lead, then this must be fixed before proceeding further. With the lead reconnected it is by no means certain that proper contact with the network will be established. It is easier to get the controlling software confused than it is to get things working again.

The normal way of re-establishing contact is to switch off the device that is giving problems, wait a few seconds, and then switch it on again. In

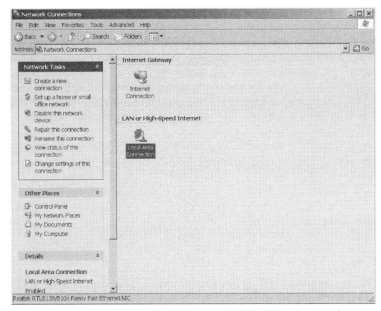

*Fig.5.18 Windows XP has a facility to repair the selected network
connection, but there is no guarantee that this will solve
the problem*

an extreme case it could be necessary to switch off everything in the
network, and then power it up again, one device at a time, starting with
the access point. Fortunately, it is very rare for the network to get into
such a state that it requires a complete restart to sort things out.

Windows XP has a repair feature that will try to re-establish contact if a
network connection fails. There is no guarantee that it will work, but
there is nothing to lose by trying it. Start by going to the Network
Connections section in the Windows Control Panel and then select the
network connection that is giving problems (Figure 5.18). In the Network
Tasks list near the top left-hand corner of the window, locate and left-
click the "Repair this connection" link. This will report that the connection
has been repaired, or give the reason that if failed to repair it, as
appropriate.

Points to remember

Many wi-fi problems have simple solutions. Particularly where no signal at all is received, look for something very basic such as a piece of equipment not being plugged in or switched on, an aerial knocked out of position, or incorrect settings in the software.

Problems with inadequate range are less likely to be encountered if the system is carefully planned rather than just being "thrown" together. The access point should be near the middle of the building. This ensures that you do not end up with the access point on the opposite side of the building to one or more wi-fi enabled units.

Ultimately there is only one way to determine whether a link can be established between the access point and each wi-fi enabled device, and that it to try it in practice. When operating well within the theoretical limits you would be very unlucky if a link operating at or close to the maximum transfer rate could not be established. Things naturally become iffier when trying to operate near the theoretical maximum range.

Changing the channel used by the network will often give an improvement with a system that is not providing the expected range. This is presumably due to some channels containing more noise than others. The default channel is channel 11, and one could reasonably expect this to be the most used, which in turn is likely give it the highest noise level. Moving away from the default channel can give noticeably better results.

The short wavelengths of wi-fi radio signals can give quite well defined "blind" spots where there is little or no reception from the access point. Moving one or both aerials will often give a strong signal and fast transfers, even if there was an inadequate signal level previously. When optimising the positions of the aerials it is very useful to have a program that gives an indication of signal strength.

Aerials do not work well when they are in very close proximity to walls, large computers, pieces of furniture, etc. Try to get the aerials where they are at least a few hundred millimetres away from any large object.

This is especially important for the access point's aerial. If the access point does not work effectively, the whole wi-fi network can not perform well. Remember that everything communicates via the access point.

Because wi-fi equipment operates at extremely high frequencies it is free from much of the electrical noise generated by household gadgets. Even so, it is advisable not to have the access point positioned right next to any electronic units, and it should definitely be positioned well away from microwave ovens.

Problems with poor performance might be due to the local environment not being conducive to good radio propagation. An improved aerial should give a significant boost in performance, and there are other options such as multiple access points and repeaters. However, it might be more practical to simply accept a slower operating speed or opt for a wired link if high speed is essential.

With problem hardware it can be necessary to uninstall and reinstall the driver software once or twice in order to get everything working properly. The instructions supplied in the installation manual are not always correct. Look on the installation disc for more up-to-date instructions.

Make sure that the adapter has the correct country setting. It might not work properly with the rest of the system if the wrong country setting is used, and it might operate in a fashion that is not legal in the UK.

Index

Index

Index